The Psychic Power
of Children

The Psychic Power of Children

By Cassandra Eason

foulsham

London•New York•Toronto

foulsham

Yeovil Road, Slough, Berkshire SL1 4JH

ISBN 0-572-02030-9
Copyright © 1994 Cassandra Eason

Designed and typeset by WightWitch Editorial Services Isle of Wight

Printed in Great Britain by St Edmundsbury Press Ltd, Bury St Edmunds, Suffolk.

Contents

By the same author

Psychic Suburbia

Rune Divination for Today's Woman
Tarot Divination for Today's Woman
I Ching Divination for Today's Woman
Crystal Divination for Today's Woman
Moon Divination for Today's Woman
Pendulum Divination for Today's Woman

A Mother's Instincts
Families Are Forever

IT IS MORE than five years since I wrote the first book on psychic children. I had originally intended to find psychological explanations for children's psychic experiences but I ended up with more questions than answers. Since then I have continued to hear many strange stories after I have given lectures or taken part in radio phone-ins around the country. Most families can recall at least one inexplicable incident involving their children, although many people are too shy to admit to them.

But I still get most experiences from people — especially mothers — whom I meet in the street, the park, the school playground and the supermarket,. Often they are women who were afraid that their experiences or those of their children were odd and they are relieved just to have a sympathetic ear.

As time goes on I find that the psychological explanations become less and less satisfactory to explain away the magical and wondrous world of childhood.

Cassandra Eason

Chapter One

News From Nowhere

I WAS IN no condition to appreciate Jack's message of doom at 9am on a Sunday morning. It had been a long night. My husband John, a journalist, had been working overnight at the breakfast television station TVam, 40 miles away in London. I had been on the night shift as well with four children, the youngest, Miranda, only a few months old and teething with a vengeance.

If my two-and-a-half-year-old son had told me the world was coming to an end I would have replied: 'That's nice, but don't talk while you're eating.'

'Daddy's gone poly-boys on his motor bike, but he's all right,' said Jack calmly and carried on with his breakfast. Poly-boys was the playful expression I used when I rolled Jack on the floor while dressing him.

'That's nice,' I replied. 'Don't poke your sister, Tom.' All I could think about was that John would soon be home and there was only another 30 minutes to survive. But John was not going to be home in 30 minutes.

As I was talking to Jack, the back wheel of John's motorcycle hit a patch of oil and he skidded helplessly on to the elevated section of the M4 motorway in west London.

The cartoons had finished and Sunday's religious programmes were failing to hold the children's attention. John should have been home ages ago. Jack's words were beginning to worry me but what could I do? Phone the police and say: 'Excuse me, my two-and-a-half-year old has told me my husband has gone poly-boys on his motorcycle . . . Yes, somewhere between London and Reading. What sort of motorcycle? Well, red with a sort of sloping pillion seat — very uncomfortable.'

I abandoned that idea and reasoned that toddlers were always predicting someone's downfall: this must be Jack's way of projecting his hostile feelings against his dad, who had perhaps denied him a second ice cream the day before. Or perhaps he was talking about something he'd seen on television.

By 11am the baby was howling, the children had eaten the entire week's supply of biscuits and, fearing the worst, I had planned the tea after the funeral service when I heard the bike and rushed out.

'I know what's happened — Jack told me,' I said looking at the battered bike and rider with a mixture of fury, relief and amazement.

John had not been killed, although he could easily have been. At that time on a Sunday morning the usually chaotic M4, the main motorway westward out of London, was not teeming with traffic. Only his pride and his beloved Honda VF750 had been hurt.

Later we discussed the incident and tried to find a rational explanation.

Was Jack a seer? Neither then nor now had he any trace of other-worldliness. He was a perfectly ordinary, scruffy, sister-baiting, noisy boy whose only accurate prophecy in the past had been: 'Daddy be cross about the sand.' (He had just shovelled the entire contents of his sand pit through the dining room window while pretending to be an excavator on a building site.)

Had it all happened as I remembered it? Memory, even for recent events, can be very unreliable and we are remarkably prone to recall as a fact what was merely suggested. Quite unconsciously, in retelling a story even a few minutes later, we add details, exclude some which we might think irrelevant and tidy up the incident, not intending fraud, but simply to try to make sense of what happened in our terms.

This has been proved in psychological experiments when subjects have watched a film of a traffic accident. It has been remarkably easy to convince the viewers that a car passed a non-existent barn or stopped at a Give Way, not a Stop sign. Less than half an hour later science students have contradicted the evidence of their own eyes. This process is intensified under real conditions of stress.

Did Jack really say that Daddy had had an accident or did he merely imply it? Had John not had an accident, would I have recalled merely an unfulfilled hint or nothing at all? After all how many times a day does a child predict something that does not come true? Any harassed mother will confirm that the figure could run into hundreds. So the occasional hit is inevitable and at the age of three, mum and dad are likely to feature a great deal in his fantasies.

Had it just been a coincidence? I was always worried about John driving home when he was very tired and perhaps Jack had voiced my fear then tried to reassure me by saying his dad would be all right.

He might have made similar remarks before that I had not consciously registered and it was only when John was late and I was searching for an explanation that I recalled this one.

But the question remains: did John at the moment of his accident send out some signal that Jack who was specially close to him picked up?

Was it some form of telepathy or clairvoyance? The accident happened on January 4, 1987. Now, seven years on, we are still not sure what happened.

Some people we told about the incident immediately seized the rational options. Others said that it was a well-known fact that children were psychic but offered little evidence for this statement. More interesting were those who, sometimes hesitantly, told us of strange occurrences involving their childhood or their children.

One of my husband's colleagues, John Keeble, was aviation correspondent with the Evening News in London in 1975 and his job often took him away from home. He was covering a story in Hong Kong when, at about two in the morning, he woke with a strong sensation that something was dreadfully wrong and he had to phone home. He eventually gave in to the impulse and phoned home to find that his son, Simon, then aged three, had caught his arm on a piece of wood while playing and trapped a splinter in the muscle. The boy was taken to hospital where he was operated on and had to stay overnight.

At that stage in his career, John was used to being away from home, and was not given to ringing up whenever he felt uneasy. But on this occasion the feeling was so strong, he could not resist it. Nothing like it has happened before or since, he says.

Until then he had been highly sceptical of the occult and allied subjects, having had to deal with numerous reports of 'flying saucers' and the like. He still feels sceptical about many aspects but this was an incident for which he could not easily find an explanation.

This story alone is not convincing proof of telepathy for most of the serious scientists who bother to deal with the subject. They demand proof from experiments which can be reproduced in a laboratory, ideally over and over again, in the same way that the laws of physics can be proved.

The most popular experiments — with the scientists if not the participants — involve telepathic 'receivers' trying to guess what cards are being turned over by telepathic 'senders'. To be of any statistical use, the cards must be turned over hundreds and hundreds of times. We hardly bothered to weigh up the possibility of engaging Jack's attention in a card turning experiment for even a few minutes before we gave up that approach.

Even if we could have got him interested, past experiments have proved that card prediction is pretty boring and that bored children can come up with some ingenious forms of cheating. The other problem is that in a laboratory there can be little of the emotional links, the hopes and fears that seem to drive this force called telepathy.

Anyway, we had no laboratory for setting up elaborate experiments. But we did have something better when John replaced the battered Honda with a BMW 650 ('German engineering is so much more solid,' he told me in an attempt to calm my fears. 'I'll be much safer'). I was still worried about accidents but I suppose from a purely scientific viewpoint I should have been glad that his love of two-wheeled transport and the number of lunatics on the road provided the possibility that history would repeat itself and Jack might get another crack at getting a message from a 'daddy going poly-boys'.

But Jack has always been perverse (he made a mockery of any experiments I tried on him while working for a degree in psychology) and having had a go at telepathy he tried something new.

In November 1988, when Miranda was almost three, but our fifth child Bill who was eight months old had filled the nightly teething spot, Jack began talking about a daddy who was having or had had a motorcycle accident. This time he did not speak as if he was picking up some strong emotion from an actual incident. It was more of a fairground prediction.

It was about seven o'clock in the evening, and he was not watching television where he might have picked up the idea, but demolishing his younger sister's Lego model. His words were vague and I was not even sure he was talking about our daddy, though he said the daddy had a beard, which ours did.

John was now working on the Guardian newspaper in London and we were still living near Reading. So I rang his office to check that he had arrived safely. He had so I asked if in his office there were any daddies, or adults that Jack might class as daddies, who had arrived in a battered state after their bike was hit by a van or lorry on a 'stiff road', near the office where there was a tower where people went up and down.

John knew of no such accidents, then, worried about his deadlines, rang off after assuring me that he would be extra careful on his way home. But, he complained, Jack's warning had been a bit light on detail. When I tried to question Jack about the crash he was remarkably uncooperative in supplying more information, obviously feeling that he had done his bit already.

'You know,' he said impatiently, 'you know!' The daddy had been hit by a lorry but had not fallen off. Was it our daddy or another daddy? 'A daddy with a beard.' Where did this happen? 'On the stiff road.' He knew perfectly well what a stiff road was and saw no reason to explain it to thick adults. It was near Daddy's work and the tower where people go up and down, of course. The ancient oracles that spoke in riddles would have been proud of him.

I could not say that Jack comes from psychic stock although my father, also a Jack, had been a great one for gloomy prophecy. 'Had a dream about a gaping grave,' he would cackle at breakfast. 'It had your name on it, so I should be careful if I were you.' This scared me as a schoolgirl but as I am still alive and kicking, my father has to be written off as a rather gloomy soul rather than a genuine prophet.

That night John arrived home later than usual, not

because the prophecy had come true, but because he had driven more carefully than usual. Though a bit of a sceptic, he admitted to taking extra care when passing several towers on his way back: the Post Office Tower, the neo-gothic architecture of St Pancras railway station, and hotel blocks near Heathrow airport just off the M4. Furthermore, though he knew there was nothing in it, he had kept a sharp lookout for lorries.

Nothing happened for the next few days so we began to wonder if by 'daddy' Jack had meant somebody else's daddy or just any grown-up. Or perhaps no one at all.

After all, we knew that the picture of a motorcycle accident was already in Jack's mind. A few weeks before, we had seen one involving a motorcyclist with a beard just like his dad.

This made quite an impression on Jack and he talked a lot about ambulances and blood and squashed people. He was not particularly upset but quite interested by the idea. This accident certainly struck a chord with me which is possibly why I took his warning more seriously.

At my insistence, John began to make inquiries about accidents at his office (discreetly as it is hardly a normal conversation piece to ask 'Had any good crashes lately? By the way, are you anybody's daddy?'). He found one incident that seemed to fit. Jim had come off his bike (admittedly a pedal cycle) when a van forced him on to ground made rough by roadworks (possibly what was meant by 'the stiff road') near St Pancras railway station (the tower?).

With a bit of stretching this could be made to fill the bill and since Jim was apparently fit and well, I felt irrationally

16

relieved. Jim was clean shaven and the accident had happened some weeks before Jack's speech so we decided that Jack had perhaps been looking into the past or had got it wrong so we could forget about it.

Some three weeks later, on Wednesday November 30, 1988, John was driving back from London along the M4 at about 70mph when he saw a bunch of slower cars ahead. He decelerated to match their speed but the butcher's van racing up behind him didn't. There was a sickening jolt as the van smacked into the back of the bike and John shot forward like a bullet from a gun.

If he had come off at that speed on the motorway in traffic he might have been killed. But he hung on and managed to brake just before hitting the cars ahead.

You could say that Jack had done it again. There had been a van or lorry in the accident and daddy had stayed on and was not hurt.

Again we tried to find the rational explanation.

Given the high number of road accidents involving motorcyclists and the number of accidents on the M4 — one of the most dangerous motorways in Britain — with John travelling twice a day, four or five times a week and usually tired, the chances of a mishap were very high. So Jack's 'gypsy's warning' had a good chance of coming true.

And what about the tower that Jack mentioned? At the scene of the accident, near the M25 interchange, the nearest towers are at Heathrow but are well out of sight. The stiff road might mean the motorway but it could mean anything: roadworks, an elevated section - you pays your money and you takes your choice. Jack at different times would say the road was where broken cars were, or the dual carriageway, but if he bothered to answer questions about it at all he just said: 'You know, the stiff road.'

Was it clairvoyance or coincidence? Laboratory experiments might have failed to come up with convincing proof of children's psychic abilities but children have traditionally been regarded as having second sight. Until the mid-nineteenth century, young boys would travel round Europe interpreting the crystal ball for their frequently fraudulent masters.

In ancient Greece, pure young boys were used for 'scrying', divining the future by gazing into bowls of pure water lit by burning torches. They studied the changes in the water in the flickering light and invoked the gods or demons to provide a meaning.

Cagliostro, the 18th century magician and adventurer, is reported to have often used young children to help him predict the future or perform acts of clairvoyance. In one famous incident, the five-year-old son of Marshal von Medem, under Cagliostro's guidance, saw the unexpected arrival home of his elder brother and was able to describe what was going on in other rooms of the house.

A vivid description of scrying with a child appears in Wilkie Collins' classic detective story, *The Moonstone*. A trio of Indian priests who are trying to retrieve a gem which was stolen from their temple take a boy from the slums, hypnotise him and make him gaze into a small pool of ink. The boy tells them by which road the carrier of the Moonstone will come but his prophecy is not wholly accurate and they fail to intercept the messenger.

Back in real life, Jack's apparent telepathic link with his

father during a time of stress is mirrored by a story told about the late Sir Peter Scott, the naturalist, painter and sailor. When he was a young child, about the time his father, Captain Scott died in the Antarctic in his bid to reach the South Pole, he is said to have told his mother: 'Daddy's stopped working.'

I asked him about the story shortly before his death in 1989 and Sir Peter wrote back: 'The story you describe was related to me in later years by my mother who was very loath to believe that it had any significance, as she was always very sceptical of psychic phenomena. But the fact that she told me the story indicates, I think, that she was unwilling to dismiss the incident.

'I'm afraid I do not recall the actual happening at all. Nor do I remember any other such phenomena in my childhood. But, as in so many other fields, I like to think I keep an open mind.'

Did the boy in fact share his father's last moments? Or did he often talk about his father, perhaps as many children do play at being his father and perhaps act out some of the anxieties that were expressed about the dangerous nature of the mission?

Sir Peter's mother, Kathleen Bruce, the sculptress who was to create the famous Peter Pan statue that stands in Kensington Gardens (J.M. Barrie, author of Peter Pan was Sir Peter Scott's godfather) had no inkling of her husband's death and it was six months before the frozen bodies of Scott and his companions were discovered.

But there is evidence that as death approached Captain Scott was thinking of his family. Among the letters he wrote during the time he was awaiting death in the snowbound tent, was one to Barrie saying: 'I want you to help my widow and my son, your godson . . . Give the boy a chance in life if the state won't do it — he ought to have good stuff in him'. In his last diary, Scott writes that he hopes the boy would be made interested in natural history rather than games. In fact, Sir Peter proved equally skilled at both.

He was certainly an exceptional person, but when I related the story of Jack I was surprised at the number of mothers of perfectly ordinary, noisy scruffy children who came out with extraordinary tales of their offspring's psychic experiences ranging from minor cases of telepathy to poltergeists.

Usually these stories are kept under cover for fear of ridicule or worse. In nearly all the stories that follow, the names have been changed and details disguised at the request of the tellers, some of whom, even years later feel insecure about discussing their experiences.

Many had gone through experiences that their parents had dismissed as just fantasy. Christine, now an adult, related that she always knew when things were going to happen but her mother would not believe that this came from any paranormal ability and accused her of listening at doors.

One child psychiatrist told me that he had never heard a child tell him about ghosts. It could be because such incidents were rare, but as he pointed out: 'The child may well not tell you things like that. The child may well be frightened that he is going mad or may be seen that way. It can worry mum who may encourage the child to keep quiet about that aspect of family life.' As one mum said:

'I just knew the psychologist would label us straight away so I told my child not to mention it.'

Dr Michael Jackson, a clinical psychologist with the University of Bangor, considers that badly-handled childhood psychic experiences can make a person withdraw from reality and perhaps lead to later mental problems. He considers that sensitive people are most likely to have such experiences and so will be even more hurt if these experiences are rejected. Certainly adults can react very negatively towards children who do not conform.

One of saddest cases I have heard of was that of Carol who, when little, used to talk to animals and people whom even her twin sister could not see. Eventually she mentioned a Red Indian chief she used to see and her parents got so worried that they had her taken to a mental hospital when she was a teenager. There she realised that if she was going to get out she had to play by the rules. She no longer mentioned the things although she kept seeing them. When she was 25 she went to a medium who told her that she was psychic and had a Red Indian guide.

Carol has never forgiven her parents for what they did.

Even now, although she holds a responsible job, her parents refuse to discuss either what happened or anything to do with her psychic experiences.

Children are much more vulnerable than adults who have learned, in Carol's phrase 'to play by the rules'. If they see what might be a ghost or experience what might be telepathy they either rationalise it or keep quiet. But children open their mouths hoping to be believed or reassured and all too often can be ignored or frightened.

Julia told me that her late mother was at a boarding

school run by nuns during the Second World War. One morning she told them she had seen a ghost in the dormitory. The nuns were furious and put her head into an unlit gas oven and then threw her into a swimming pool with her clothes on saying that was what happened to wicked girls who told lies. Julia says that after that incident her mother closed her mind to the psychic which meant that Julia could never talk about her own experiences as a child. While that is a very extreme case children's psychic experiences can prove a stumbling block for some teachers.

Indeed one of Jack's first teachers asked me if Jack could predict the winner of the 3.30 at Aintree. Another school wouldn't allow me to interview children about ghosts as the Head Teacher felt it might frighten the children. Yet the Junior Department sent an invitation home shortly afterwards to watch my children perform a play called *Spooksville* complete with ghouls eating vampire burgers and spectres in white sheets rattling chains.

Perhaps one of the problems is that teachers do not meet the issue at college. In particular, those who do not have children can be fazed by having a child say he or she has seen a dead relative. As a self-assured young teacher for ten years I never heard a psychic experience. As a mother it is very different.

Six-year-old Sarah lost her young brother from leukaemia but continued to see him and play with him. She got a sympathetic reception at home because her mum too had vivid dreams about Ben and had felt his presence many times. So when she saw Ben at school she dashed to tell Mrs Jones her teacher, a kind, experienced middle-aged woman.

But as Sarah blurted out her story her teacher turned her round very gently, propelled her out of the room and shut the door. Sarah was puzzled. She later told her mother: 'I saw Ben. He was in Assembly with me. The girl next to me couldn't see him but I moved over to give him space.'

'What was he wearing?' her mother asked.

'Oh not exactly purple, those lilac coloured shorts and a Jason Donovan top in lilac patterns with a hood.'

Just before five year old Ben had died his mother had bought him a new lilac Jason top and shorts in the town where Ben was in hospital. Ben had died suddenly and his mother had pulled the unworn clothes from the top of the case and put them on Ben for the funeral. So Sarah had never seen the clothes and her mum certainly hadn't talked about them to anyone.

'What was he wearing on his feet?' her mother asked.

'Oh I couldn't see because he was flying.'

Mrs Jones isn't the only teacher to have problems in dealing with the psychic. Jessica, a teacher in Hertford-shire told me about her dilemma: 'A family came to the school whom we heard had a lot of trouble with the police where they used to live, mainly involving some cousins. The oldest boy who was eight and in my class seemed very tense and behaved oddly. Then he started to draw ghosts and to talk about a thing in his house that threw plates and smashed things.

'Tim became progressively afraid of what was happening at home. I didn't know what to do and so I tried to talk to the Headmistress about the problem. But she told me on no account must I encourage Tim to talk about what was happening and should change the subject if he mentions it. I didn't want to go against her but I kept an eye on the lad. Things got worse at home and so did his behaviour. I wonder if we should have intervened.

'One morning he told me that a Vicar had been to the house and the thing had gone. Tim's behaviour improved dramatically, But now I have Jimmy, Tim's younger brother in my class and recently he has become tense and difficult. Jimmy too has started to draw ghosts and I don't know what to do. We were concerned to hear that the four children had been locked in their room and I know there has been violence in the family. But no-one will talk about the poltergeist though I fear it is starting up again.'

The adult code of silence extends even to people connected with organisations which investigate the paranormal. They have told me stories about psychic experiences of their childhood or that of their relatives then quickly said: 'But if you use it, don't mention my name as it's not fair to my family.'

Telepathy, ghosts and things that go bump in the night are fine in ghost tales. In everyday life, they can start off all sort of ripples which can be a real threat to the picture of the safe old world sanitised and technologically in order.

Children already cause enough disorder in everyday life as any parent or aunt or uncle knows. Mix them with the paranormal and the results can be shattering. When I started off to write a nice neat book about the psychic world of children I found that the stories I gathered would not fit into nice neat packages any more than children will fit into their nice neat clothes on those important occasions when you want them to look their best.

Children's psychic experiences start where fantasy begins and end — who knows where? For that reason, I have recorded some of the borderline stories of children's invisible friends and night terrors. Readers must make up their own minds which side of the boundaries of imagination they lie.

More often than not the children themselves cannot distinguish between the paranormal and fantasy and may accept the verdict of adults that they have been dreaming. Only in later life do they look back and say 'I didn't realise at the time, but it was not mere fantasy as I was told, but was an actual psychic experience'.

For some old people those magic moments of childhood have proved to be more important than the rest of their lives put together. For that reason I have included their reminiscences.

Also included are the stories of adults who have had paranormal experiences involving children. For children do not live alone and often their 'magic' can rub off on mothers, fathers, relatives — and even teachers.

I have written about ordinary people with ordinary kids who have had out-of-the-ordinary things happen to them. I also consulted the archives at the Alister Hardy Research Centre in Oxford and the International Association for Near Death Studies at Northleach and to see just how widespread the phenomena was.

Before my own experience with Jack I would have been tempted to discard many of the stories I came across as an insult to common sense. Now I feel that they need more careful study and have included them for other people's consideration. Names and details have been changed, as requested by the people I spoke to and the institutes, to protect the tellers from scorn or sightseers.

In updating and revising this book I have left many of original cases that have stood the test of time that I know have proved helpful to readers but have added many new ones. Above all I found that many parents do need advice and reassurance as to how to deal with their children's psychic lives and so I've added practical suggestions that other mums and dads have given to me — plus a few that I've used in my own family life and in advising people who have phoned me or written for help.

The psychic powers of children are quite normal, very common and can enrich the lives of adults around them. And the wisdom and insight of our children can remind us of what really matters and that life is a very special, wonderful gift to be cherished and enjoyed.

Chapter Two

A Psychic SOS

JACK'S LITTLE BIT of telepathy involving his motor-cycling father (we have not yet been able to come up with a better explanation for this incident) occurred at a moment of stress for the family and for John.

Telepathy under stress is a difficult subject to study systematically because crises cannot happen to order and certainly not just to oblige the ever-eager psychologist or scientist with their meters and boxes of tricks.

It is possible to look at the experiences, to talk to those involved, find out something of the context in which the events occurred and to look at underlying feelings. These experiences usually seem to involve close relatives. Do children's minds become attuned so that a physical presence is not necessary to communicate in times of strong emotions and a kind of psychic SOS is sent out?

During the retreat to Dunkirk, in the last world war,

Michael, a young army officer was killed. Back home, in the countryside near Ipswich, his daughter, Fiona was living with her grandmother, aunts and mother. She told them: 'Daddy came to me last night and told me to take care of mummy.' Next day, a telegram brought the news that her father had been killed.

Stories of premonitions and visitations abound in times of war when there is also the increased probability of a child's fears of a parent's death, voiced at random, becoming reality. When father is away, the prospect of the telegram is not a vague fantasy. Children pick up chance remarks, unspoken glances, and unfinished sentences. They may project fears about who will take care of mummy into dreams — perhaps not remembered, perhaps not reported, perhaps not always heard by adults. We do not often attend to what children say. When we do it can be a shock.

Tim Haigh, the editor of *Psychic News,* believes that as a child he saved his mother's life through his telepathic link with her. 'When I was about 11 years old and living in a large house with my family in Yorkshire, my mother was, at that time, developing her mediumistic abilities.

'She awoke one night sensing an extremely malevolent presence around her bed. Paralysed with fear she told me later she could not even shout to wake up my father. On the other side of the house I was having a vivid and disturbing dream in which my mother was being chased around my school playground by a large ferocious dog.

'I remember getting out of bed, running along the corridor to my parents' bedroom and shouting, "The dog is after you. Are you all right, Mum?"

'It was as though I was a detached observer of the whole scene. I felt as though I was watching events rather than participating in what turned out to be, for want of a better phrase, a psychic rescue. For as soon as I entered the bedroom the malignant and abrasive presence that had built up simply disappeared and my mother was able to free herself.

'Apparently I simply turned round and went back to bed not mentioning it in the morning or for years after. It was only in later life that my mother reminded me of what happened. Then hazy memories of that night re-surfaced in my own consciousness.

'Whether it was coincidence or not, my mother is convinced I saved her life that night so perhaps there are grounds for accepting Cassandra Eason's view that there is a strong intuitive link between mother and child.'

As with Jack and Tim most crisis child telepathy is rooted in the parental/child relationship and is based on love and need. The telepathy is a two-way traffic and we cannot say whether the power originates in the child or parent. However, any people who never had a psychic experience since their own childhood do find that, on becoming parents, they become open once again to psychic abilities.

Even a young child can pick up on a brother or sister's last moments however much the adults involved try to hide the truth. Brenda who lives in Andover told me that she was about three when her twenty-month-old brother George died: 'We lived in a very poor district and tuberculosis was rampant. My little brother was in a sanitorium. One morning my gran was looking after me while my parents were visiting when I suddenly stopped playing and told her, "George is in King Jesus's garden now."

' "No," said my Nan, "he's in hospital but he's going to get better one day." But I still insisted, "No, he's with King Jesus picking flowers in his garden."

'When my mum and dad came home they told my nan my brother had died while they were with him at the time I had said. Nan confirmed the story years later but I can still remember Nan desperately trying to keep me round the back on the day of the funeral and how I insisted on pushing my dolls' pram round to the street at the moment the hearse pulled up. Dad took me to look in a toyshop window while Mum and Nan were in church.'

It doesn't have to be a blood relation whose distress a child picks up though it is usually someone they have a strong relationship with. Jan explained: 'A year ago my fiance, Paul, electrocuted himself and was taken to hospital. Fortunately my two daughters were staying overnight with a friend and knew nothing of the accident.

'When they got home Paul was there, although pretty shaken. As she came through the door my seven-year-old, Elise, said, "I had a funny dream about Paul last night. He was in a room with wires on his chest. The strange thing was he had pyjamas that colour," and she pointed to a turquoise cushion. Paul had been given turquoise hospital pyjamas as there had been no time to get anything of his own.

'It's not the first experience my daughter has had. Elise was not born while my mother was alive and yet she has seen her. She calls her 'my lady in the sky' and has described her in detail. Elise says the lady comes at Christmas and on birthdays to give her a kiss.'

Some women say they wake the second before their baby cries and 'sit bolt upright in bed', though they may sleep through an older child's yells. Or they will sense that the baby is in distress. Yet these women were not telepathic or psychic before their child's birth.

The difference appears to be that they are linked to a child and because they are not yet fully emotionally or psychologically separate, the baby can transmit his or her psychic energy to and through his mother so she can, for a brief time share his magic. What is commonly disregarded as just a mother/baby thing may be one of the most exciting psychic stages.

The mother's 'ability' seems to relate only to her and the baby, though in some cases the bond appears to remain with one particular child even into adulthood. The baby can and regularly does communicate his needs to his mother through channels that are beyond normal communication. How this works is not fully understand but it does seem to work.

When Daniel was seven-and-a-half-months-old, Janette remembers: 'My husband had closed Daniel's bedroom door because he was running a bath and the noise of the water would have woken Daniel. He had his bath and I went to run mine .

'As I passed the bedroom door I had the overwhelming feeling that I had to go to Daniel. So even thought the taps were full on and the tank was filling noisily I went straight in to find him choking. He couldn't even cry because he couldn't get enough breath in. We managed to get him to the casualty department of the local hospital. They were able to ventilate him and gave him intravenous antibiotics which fortunately worked quite quickly because his throat was closing due to a serious acute respiratory tract infection. We stayed in hospital five days and came out on Christmas Eve, the best Christmas present we ever had.'

An American, Lucille Hurd, provides another example of a mother feeling her child's distress, even 3,000 miles away on the other side of the United States. Her dad used to drive passengers across America. 'He invited me and mom to come with him but it involved travelling 600 miles a day for 30 days and mom had made the crossing at another time, but hated it.' This was Lucille's third trip and she and her grandfather and father were sitting in the front with three passengers in the back. 'On the journey to California, the car went off the road and turned over — I thought at that terrifying moment of my mother three thousand miles away in Baltimore. Next morning we phoned her from Yakima and the instant she heard my voice, she cried, ''How are you? My God, I saw you turned over in a ditch in my dream. Are they treating you well in the clinic?'' '

The passengers in the back seat were hurt and had to stay in hospital. But Lucille, her father and grandfather were only shaken and were discharged from hospital almost straight away.

A child's psychic ability first appears in early infancy it seems, though at this stage mum seems to use it for the child as an automatic psychic radar, monitoring danger the child is totally unaware of. By far most numerous childhood early experiences do involve the mother/ child link and need to be seen in this context. We need to use an interactional psychic approach to understand much early telepathy.

My book, *A Mother's Instincts* (Aquarian, 1992) traces how this bond can survive till the child is adult and perhaps a parent.

Mischievous toddlers, too, may need mum to operate their psychic protection. Eileen is now a grandma. When she was a young mother she lived over a baker's shop in Ventnor on the Isle of Wight with her two small boys. She told me: 'When Stuart was eighteen months old and Paul was three we were living on the upper two storeys of a very tall building. I went up to my bedroom to fetch something and then started to go downstairs. I'd left Stuart fast asleep in his cot in the room next door and there wasn't a sound.

'Suddenly as I was half-way down the stairs I had the most dreadful feeling Stuart was in danger. I dashed into Stuart's room to find the last bit of his leg disappearing over the window-sill.

'Somehow he'd managed to get out of his cot which he'd never done before, climbed up to the slightly open window — it was stifling especially over the baker's shop - and squeezed his way through the gap. I nailed the window up right then but if I hadn't gone to Stuart at that moment he would have been killed.'

Janette recalls how when her second son, Damien, was about four, her husband took him and his six-year-old brother Daniel to the swimming pool.

'After about 30 minutes, I looked at the clock. It was

2.48pm and I had a feeling something had happened to Damien. I remember I kept thinking of him with a bandage round his forehead. As time wore on, I was quite convinced he'd bumped his forehead. When they returned later, Damien got out of the car with a sort of white netting bandage like a cap but almost falling over his eyes. He had cracked the back of his head open on a metal bar and had 12 stitches, but being on the back of his head they had to bandage right round to keep the dressing in place. The time the accident happened, my husband said, was nearly ten to three.'

Jan, from Reading in Berkshire, told me about two experiences of telepathy involving her sons. She was working as a swimming teacher and on Thursdays would stay late at school while a friend took her children home and gave them tea. But one particular Thursday, Jan had an urgent feeling that she should go home early. It was so acute, she says, that she would have walked out if her supervisor had not agreed to let her go.

At about 1.25pm when Jan was telling her supervisor, 'Look I can't stay tonight', her son Ian, then 10, fell badly on the ice at his school some miles away and sustained a hairline fracture. The school, not realising how badly he was hurt, did not send him home and even allowed him to go to sleep, a dangerous thing to do in a case of concussion.

The friend who took him home was astonished to see Jan's car draw up at the same time she arrived. 'What are you doing here?' she asked in amazement and relief, as Ian was looking very poorly. 'I think I know what I'm doing here,' replied Jan. Ian was taken to hospital and stayed there for two days. As with cases of telepathy I have previously mentioned, Jan had changed her course without logical reason and had been there to offer her support to her distressed and badly injured child.

Jan had another experience with her elder son, Robert, when he was 14. She can date it precisely to Tuesday June 13, 1989, as he was then due to have a TB inoculation at school. Jan had an appointment at 11 am but Robert had no idea at what time he would be given the injection. Jan's visitor arrived 10 minutes late and as he walked through the door, Jan grabbed her arm and said 'ouch' for no apparent reason.

That night she asked Robert if the injection hurt. 'Did it hurt, mum!' he replied. 'I'll say it did. Ten past eleven exactly they did it. I was looking at my watch all the time to see how many seconds it took.'

Even as children get older, mums can receive a psychic call for help. Esther told me: 'Pete was ten and had made lots of friends on the French camp site where we were staying. He was off playing when I had the most terrible feeling that he was in danger and I must find him. I'd seen him only ten minutes before with his friends and he'd been quite happy. Automatically I went away from the usual places he usually played to a far corner of the site. I just "knew" he would be there. Then I caught sight of him. He was being frightened by a much older boy so I was able to intervene.'

But the psychic link can pick up good news too. A psychologist, Dr Michael Jackson, who lives in Bethesda in Wales, told me: 'When my wife Sonia was in labour with our second child we went to the hospital at nine in the morning, leaving our three -year -old son, Sammy with a babysitter. At one minute past ten at night Sammy told the babysitter that his baby brother had been born. That was the exact time the baby was born at the hospital but we had not rung through with the news.'

The messages need not always be about death and disaster but can surface perhaps at times of domestic crises. Sisters may have a special bond. Doris was fourteen and taking care of her younger sisters who were eleven and seven, while their mother had gone shopping. The house was one of the old back-to-back type in Salford with a black kitchen range and an open fire in the living room.

'My mother would often leave a pan to cook on the fire. I went upstairs, leaving my sisters together. I heard my middle sister call my name with great urgency. As my name was called I saw what was taking place downstairs — the pan of soup on the fire had been knocked by my youngest sister and the contents were pouring over her legs. I came down the stairs finding what I had expected, pulled my sister away from the fire as she still sat there shocked and in pain.

'Afterwards the middle girl remarked that I had not asked her what had happened, but simply came down and did what was necessary. She asked me how I had known.'

Had Doris not acted so promptly, the situation could have been far worse. The argument for some kind of telepathy has to be balanced by the argument that often certain dangers are in the back of one's mind at all times and that a call for help can invoke the reaction 'Oh Lord, I knew that would happen!' Doris must have had at the back of her mind the dangers of the range. What is interesting is the calm way in which she reacted, not panicking as many would do if their worst fears were confirmed. 'Seeing' the situation might have helped her stay cool.

Doris added to this story about a year after the book was first published: 'My sisters started to recall the event and things came up that I had forgotten. Apparently the youngest one had just had her hair washed and was sitting drying it while my mother went out shopping. She had a towel on her head which fell over her face and so could not see the pan of soup and she knocked it over.'

Jo from Marlborough in Wiltshire told me that his grandmother, when she was a child, knew her brother's fate by some means that we cannot yet explain. 'In 1848 when part of North Italy was ruled over by the Austrians my maternal grandmother lived in Carinthia in the South of Austria where she had been born. She was about 11 years old. Her elder brother was doing his military service and was being used to round up and put Italian soldiers, who had rebelled against Austria, up against the wall and shoot them.

'He hated doing this and without telling his family, determined to desert and emigrate to the United States. Northern Italy was about 100 miles away from his family but my grandmother suddenly exclaimed: "I see Franz. I see him getting on a boat."

'Her brother later became a Catholic priest in New York. My mother told me that story about her mother many times when I was young.'

The bond between siblings can be even stronger. James E. Peron, Director of the Childbirth Education

Foundation in the United States, told me: 'I grew up with identical twin cousins eight months older than myself. I witnessed psychic communication between these brothers as a regular occurrence. Perhaps the most startling experience was when we were about 11 years old. We had been playing with neighbouring children in their farm barn climbing to the upper beams of the barn and jumping into the hayloft. My cousin Dick and I returned home for evening meal but Donny remained playing with the neighbours' boys.

'We were sitting down at the dinner table when Dick suddenly bolted in his chair, screamed in pain and yelled, "Donny's hurt! He fell backwards from the high beam in the barn and hurt his leg."

'We rushed to the neighbouring farm, Donny had fallen at the precise moment that Dick had screamed and had broken his leg rather severely. This was but one of many such experiences I witnessed with the boys. It was comical when we played Hide and Seek — they always knew where the other was hiding. My wife and I have witnessed this same psychic ability with our own twin sons who just turned 22 years of age on November 5.'

Chapter Three

Beware of the Mini-mind Patrol

IT IS THE sense of urgency of certain experiences which separates what are apparently telepathic feelings from other less specific anxieties. But there is a second kind of telepathy which can take place in a completely relaxed situation, often when parent and child are travelling together. However, the child, having seen what is in the parent's mind might well demand urgent action. And that is when the trouble starts.

Carla Randall from Leeds has four children. She remembers pushing the baby in the buggy with Dylan, then about four, trotting along beside her. As they walked she was thinking of getting home putting on her old but very comfortable red cord trousers and cycling round to her mothers without the children so that she could get a bit of peace and quiet. 'I was at the crossroads and had a clear picture of myself riding back that way to mum's,' she said.

It would have been nice. But at that point Dylan piped up: 'Mum, why are you going on your bike in your red trousers to see nan and not taking me?'

The limpet has much to learn from the average toddler about togetherness. When I first wrote this book I rarely had a bath without Bill and Miranda joining me, Jack hurling toy ducks and Tom and Jade popping in and out chatting or demanding I referee the latest dispute.

Now with two adolescents as well as three younger ones I can rarely get into the bathroom and look back on such days with nostalgia. Is it any wonder that children can anticipate our every word and potential movement? Yet Dylan not only knew mum was planning to make a bid for freedom, he pictured the bike and the cords at the moment Carla did.

Travel featured in several experiences which were related to me, as did a state of relaxed silence between the transmitter and receiver. In 1964, Doris was sitting on a train in Manchester with her four-year-old daughter Susan on their way to see Doris's mother.

'We were waiting for the train to leave the station,' said Doris. 'Susan was looking at a comic and I was daydreaming. We were silent. My thoughts went to a journey I had made years before at the time I was living in a house at Bosham Bay in Sussex. I had been on a trip to London and my feet were tired.

'On arriving at Bosham station, I took off my shoes to walk home. Now sitting on the train in Manchester all those years later, I recalled the exact sensation of walking down the bay road without shoes and the feel of the road under my stockinged feet. Susan looked up from her comic. "Why do you never let me walk down the road without shoes?" she asked.'

Judith from Guildford, Surrey, had a similar experience. 'I'd met a friend for a pub lunch and we were driving home with my young daughter, Emma, when we passed a man standing by a hedge. I thought to myself that he must be having a leak but it turned out his car had broken down though we didn't stop. I didn't say a word about this to my daughter.

'The following day we were out in the car again on the same stretch of road and Emma asked me, "Mummy, where's that man?"

'I asked: "What man?"

' "The man you thought was having a wee-wee".'

Jeanne Langford of Guernsey has had experience of telepathy on the move and at home. The first was when she had just moved to Guernsey from London and William, their first born was three years old.

'I had received a letter from my friend and neighbour in London and she had mentioned a woman whom she thought I knew : "Simon's mother," she added. I could not think who she meant and kept saying to myself, entirely in my head:"Simon, who is Simon?"

'I had not actually uttered a word when William, who was in the same room, said to me, "You know Simon mummy. He was my friend." '

On the second occasion she was in the back of the car with their second son, Thomas, who was four. Their third child had been born and she was thinking to herself about the possibility of a fourth child when Thomas piped up: 'Would four be enough mummy?'

41

'Four what?' she asked, somewhat startled. 'Four children, of course,' he replied.

'I know that on neither of these occasions had I voiced my thoughts aloud,' she told me, 'although I was thinking in word form and the thoughts were very simple. So if the potential for telepathy is there these conditions were probably ideal for it. On other occasions I have suspected that something was going on, but the evidence was not so clear. I have also tried to make it happen but have never succeeded as far as I know.'

Jeanne is certain that she did not voice her thoughts aloud but some parents drop into the habit of keeping up a running commentary of their actions (like their children do) and do not realise they are doing it.

'Oh look! A train!' I once loudly informed the startled passengers on a bus. The problem was that I had forgotten that for once I did not have a child with me to tell about the train. One executive I know announced at a board meeting when coffee was wheeled in: 'Oh good, bickies!'

It may help children learn to talk but it also means that unconsciously many parents carry on a kind of burble without realising and can impart information to the child. Then they are amazed when he or she knows their 'secret' thoughts.

The other interesting point that Jeanne raises is that when she deliberately tried to use telepathy the children could not or would not cooperate which is bad news for the scientific community.

As I mentioned in the first chapter a lot of experiments have been carried out to test for telepathic ability in children. When the results have not been poor they have demonstrated the ingenuity of children in devising amazing codes of sniffs, shuffles, coughs and chair-creaking in the interests of improving their results, if only to get the whole thing over and done with.

For surely nothing could be more galling for a child who can pick up thoughts which are relevant to his life to find in a laboratory setting that he hasn't the foggiest idea what card his partner in crime may be selecting.

Dr Ernesto Spinelli, a psychologist living in London, did carry out some tests with children as young as three that seemed to show that small children had considerable telepathic powers. He found that three-year-olds did best of all, but the apparent ability declined from then on until at the age of eight, the results, like those of adults, were the same as chance guessing. No one else has managed to get the same results.

Perhaps the real difference between Dr Spinelli's work and that of other researchers in this field, was that he made his tests appealing to kids, with brightly coloured thinking boxes, puppets with thinking caps and thinking caps for the children to wear.

His interpretation of these experiments would seem to make sense of some real life events. Dr Spinelli thinks that telepathic powers come from the same source as ordinary thought but that in the young child, this ability has not been suppressed by learning. Telepathic power, he believes, is a sort of externalised thinking that disappears once the child learns to do his thinking inside his head.

As parents know, young children chatter away incessantly. 'Now I'm going upstairs, now I'm sitting on the toilet — oh, dear, missed! Mummy will be cross — I know

I'll wipe it up with my tee-shirt.'

Dr Spinelli found that results were best when the children guessing together were the same age and even better, when their IQs were the same. His results were just as good whether the children chose the target picture or it was selected for them using random numbers.

Commenting on the relaxation factor involved in real life telepathy he told me: 'My own feelings are that this is linked with the limitations of self-consciousness that are typically imposed, but which become more blurred when one is in a relaxed, meditative or altered state.

Since young children are only just beginning to have a clearly defined and restrictive sense of self, it is possible that their superior ability at telepathic tasks is a reflection of their open self-consciousness. Telepathy only strikes us as odd or unusual because we have a sense of self-consciousness. A notion that our thoughts are ours and ours alone.'

His experiments were carried out nearly 20 years ago. Since then more people have been interested in finding fault with his work rather than building on it and investigating a potentially very rich field.

Tasha from Oxfordshire was fourteen when I spoke to her. On several occasions she had felt that she and her father could read each other's minds.

Once they were in the car together and, as Tasha told me: 'I was wondering if some friends, Malcolm and Maxie, were coming to the barbecue. I didn't say anything. I was just thinking, when out of the blue dad said, "No, I don't think so. Mum forgot to invite them".'

In some children, telepathic ability is not restricted to

family but can extend, at random, to complete strangers. Adam who is twelve told me: 'When I was ten, I was on the tube in London with my mum. There was a big man standing next to me. I asked him where he came from and he said America.

'Then I asked him if he played a flute and he was amazed. "Yes," he said, "how did you know?" I said I just did.' Adam says there were no apparent signs that the man was a musician. It is hard to imagine a non-verbal cue that would have narrowed down the instrument that the man played, even had he been humming or tapping out a rhythm with his feet.

Another time Adam was at the Chalk Pits in Hampshire where he had gone to see a band called the Bhundu Boys. A man next to him boasted that he was psychic and could tell fortunes. Adam had heard the man say to his friend that he had a boat and decided to have a bit of fun.

'You've got a boat,' he said.

'Yes,' replied the man, 'But what colour is it?'

'Blue and white,' said Adam, without knowing how he had come to the correct answer. This might have been just a lucky guess. Blue and white is a fairly common colour combination for boats. But he went on to tell the man he had a former girlfriend called Emma who was interested in politics. The so-called psychic was amazed and told Adam to go on, but he couldn't.

Though such mind-hopping is most common with young children some teenagers retain the ability, especially when they have a good relationship with parents, although this can sometimes be difficult in the teenage years. Dads in particular seem to score well as psychic partners. Perhaps teenagers are more consciously trying to move away from mum.

Hugh was 13 and at school in Liphook in Hampshire when, at the end of the summer term, his father cycled up to see him from their home in Southampton which was 30 miles away. 'My father told me, "I've found you a bicycle cape just like the one you wanted. I was cycling along and found it in front of me in the road. So I got off and picked it up."

'I replied, Let me tell you where you found it. You were cycling up Weston Road away from our house towards the Avenue and it was opposite the waste ground where the house has been pulled down and you found it about a yard from the curb."

' "How did you know?" my father asked.

'I had visualised the incident as he was telling me but at the same time I felt sure that I was picturing what had actually happened.'

As a last resort telepathy can be useful to keep mum on the straight and narrow if she's up to anything illicit — like having 40 winks which is definitely not playing the game in children's eyes. Esther told me: 'I had a bad night's sleep and wasn't feeling well so I had dropped asleep in the chair one afternoon. Suddenly I woke to hear eight-year-old Dean calling me. I rushed to the door thinking I'd over-slept and he'd come home alone though I'd promised to be there to meet him outside school. But he wasn't at the door. When I looked at the clock it was the right time to go and fetch him but he'd obviously thought he'd better remind me.'

Telepathy is primarily then a link of love. If we get a

telepathic warning about or from a child we should obey the psychic call. It can be a life-saver or at least protect our child from distress. Routine telepathy is a sign of how special our children are and that we should value magical relationship.

We don't need to have psychic guessing games with our children. Indeed these links of love happen most where a child isn't pressurised by constant activities. In the quietness of a walk together or just sharing time without canned entertainment magic is at its strongest. Kids need space and approval to develop all their natural abilities, psychic and otherwise.

I said in the first chapter that children's psychic experiences do not come in neat packages. What can we conclude from the story told by Tanya Garland of how another child apparently communicated psychically with her to tell her that her daughter was drowning? An observant and quick-witted toddler? Yes, but according to his mother, he couldn't talk at the time he communicated the danger to Tanya.

Tanya explained: 'When we lived in Tonga my daughter and I were on the beach with my friend's two year old boy. There was a coral reef with live coral. It was possible to walk on it though it was very spiky. It was very worn with lots of potholes. There were shallow pools on it when the tide was in and the children would run along on it like a playground and then jump into the pools. I was sitting with some other parents on the beach. I thought it was safe, not realising there were any deep potholes. But on this occasion my daughter who was three, jumped into one that was about four foot deep.

'She and the girl she was playing with disappeared. The women were in deep conversation so we didn't notice anything, But the little boy saw it happen and said very clearly to me, "The girls are drowning."

'I heard him, looked up and could not see the girls. I shouted to the other women for help as I rushed down the beach. I found the girls and pulled them out. The other girl had fallen on top of my daughter who was trapped at the bottom of the hole. I held my daughter upside down until she breathed and then rushed her to hospital.

'Later I said to the boy's mother, "Your son saved my daughter's life when he called out and told me the girls were drowning.

' "That's impossible," said his mother. "He can't speak yet." She laughed at me and she wouldn't believe me.'

Another incident of a child showing unexpected abilities in a time of crisis was related to me by Rosanne who lives in Telford. Her son, Nicklas, was only three at the time and, in his mother's words, 'rather a slow developer who had had problems in his speech and comprehension'. But he came to the rescue when his mother, Rosanne, suffered a severe diabetic attack while they were alone together at home. Rosanne had collapsed and was lying on the floor, unable to move and knowing that she would soon lapse into a coma. It was vital that Nicklas brought her the phone so she could summon help while she was still able to talk.

Parents know the near-impossibility of getting a toddler to co-operate at the best of times. They are just as likely to scream or wander off — or just ignore you.

Rosanne just managed to slur the words 'Get Mummy

phone' and Nicklas ran to the telephone and touched it. but the cord was tangled around the table leg.

Somehow he understood what he had to do and, frowning with concentration, he began to unthread the tangled cord while Rosanne looked on helplessly. At last he brought her the phone but her fingers were now too numb to dial her husband's work number. She took his hand and willed him to poke out one tiny finger which she guided towards the buttons.

Somehow the number was dialled and she managed to mumble 'Terry' to her husband's secretary. But the secretary recognised her voice and help came before she lapsed into what her doctor told her would have been a fatal coma.

How had Nicklas performed so remarkably well in the crisis? Did Rosanne, in her desperation, manage to break through to him telepathically or did he draw upon untapped and apparently undeveloped resources of his own in the desire to save his mother?

Does this sound fanciful? But it was not the only time that Nicklas showed some form of psychic power. His grandfather died when he was three but when he was six he started to talk about his 'guard' and said that his grandfather lived inside him. 'Sometimes,' Rosanne told me, 'he would go into a corner and start talking to his grandfather who seemed to act as his guardian angel.'

Many children have invisible friends and we shall look at them in a later chapter. But while many such invisible friends can be dismissed as fancy, this one helped to find Rosanne's stolen car.

'Nicklas came to me in the garden and said that his guard knew where the car was. He kept going across the lawn and apparently talking into thin air, listening and then coming back to me. He said there were two bridges and the car was by the first bridge. There were a lot of shops not far away and sometimes we went to the place for a picnic and there was a special church I had been to. When I suggested several places, Nicklas got annoyed and said it was where cars went over and under the bridges. I put it down to an overactive imagination.

'When the car was found it was on a slip road just off a dual carriageway. There were two bridges nearby. The car was by the first bridge. A couple of miles back was Telford shopping centre and the park, where we had had a couple of picnics. Not far to the right of the place was the Spiritualist church that I had attended a couple of times since my father died. But how did Nicklas know?'

Chapter Four

Facing the Future

JACK'S PREDICTION ABOUT the motorcycle and the stiff road was a one-off like most children's predictions that I have come across. The average child is and should be far too busy enjoying today to give thought to tomorrow. What is more, young children have usually forgotten a premonition however world-shattering by the time the event occurs.

When my youngest son Bill was two years old we were in the bedroom of our Reading semi when Bill trotted to the window and said with interest, 'Fire in the sky'. It was quite a low window and he was pointing over the house-tops. But I could see nothing. Next day he called me up to the bedroom again to see 'the fire in the sky'. This continued for about a week. Then a bakery caught fire about a mile and a half distant and the sky was filled with smoke and flames in the area Bill had shown me. I rushed upstairs to show him his fire in the sky but he wasn't especially interested as he was playing with some new Lego. He had completely forgotten his words.

Yet in some cases children's premonitions can be lifesavers if we listen to them. Kate, who lives in Wiltshire was about 13 and very interested in CB radio, when she had her glimpse of the future. 'I was going to an event and some friends were giving me a lift to Trowbridge. Suddenly I had the most dreadful premonition that if I stayed in the car there would be an accident or something dreadful would happen to me. So I said, 'Can you drop me off and I'll give you a call on the CB in half and hour?'

'They did though they must have thought I was behaving oddly. Half an hour later I tried to get through on the radio but there was nothing on their waveband. About three quarters of an hour later I made contact with the boys' mum and discovered the car had overturned and a tree had toppled over and gone through the back seat. The boys were all right but had I been in the back seat I would have been killed.'

Even if an accident can't be prevented some people believe that the effects can be lessened by prayer and that this is the point of predictive dreams or visions as Jackie, who lives in San Diego in California, discovered. 'My landlady's 10-year-old daughter Lucy came to me and told me about a vivid dream that had frightened her. In the dream she had been badly injured in a car accident and her mother was crying over her.

'Lucy wanted to know if it would really happen. I told her I thought if she prayed that perhaps she could prevent it. A year later I took Lucy and her sister for a drive as I occasionally did. Their parents didn't own a car. But as I travelled along the four-lane freeway I saw suddenly ahead in the third lane that, right on a curve, someone had abandoned a car with neither flares nor direction signals. Seconds before my attention had been diverted by another car suddenly slowing up and pulling off the road.

'It was too late to swerve because the other lanes were full, so I braked as hard as I could. I slid and hit the back end on my driver's side so hard it bent the front seat into a V and I could hardly get out. But I only had a skinned elbow. Lucy had a skinned knee and her sister a sprained thumb. They were in the back seat. A third car ran into mine and had a crashed fender.

'The crash stopped traffic in all four lanes as far as you could see.

'No one who saw the wreckage could believe we had walked away alive. I think Lucy's prayer was most definitely answered.'

It might seem wonderful to be able to foresee the future but it can have unpleasant side effects. Often the messenger gets the blame for bringing bad news as Pat found out.

'When I was 13,' she told me, 'it was the first time one of my dreams had ever come true. I woke up and did not want my breakfast. "What's the matter with you?" mum asked in her usual brisk way. "I had an awful dream someone was at the bottom of the pool," I said meaning the small lake in the town.

'Mum sent me off to school and told me not to be stupid.

'When I got home the door was locked. It was never locked so I was worried. I knocked and mum opened it. I will never forget her words. "Your bloody dream," she said. Her cousin had drowned in the pool that day. Her sight was failing and she had mistaken the algae growing round the edge of the pool for grass and had walked on it. It was 40 years ago, but I can still remember how terrified I was and how furious my mother was. "Your bloody dream," she said.'

Even pleasant predictions can misfire. Dorothy, now a grandmother, can remember when she was 14 going to a dancing club with her mother. There she told a friend of her mother: 'You are going to win the raffle.' The prediction was correct but Dorothy found herself the target of a lot of anger because everyone thought the raffle had been fixed.

Joy from McKinleyville, in the United States told me the story of her Aunt Florence who was born in Nebraska in 1887. 'When Florence was about 13, she attended a sporting games day at her little school. They all sat in makeshift bleachers [raised stalls] to watch. Girls in those days were so prim and Victorian you couldn't believe it. Florence, being pretty, was especially afraid to call any attention to herself.

'In the middle of the game, Florence leaped up, shouted "Run" at the top of her little voice, ran and dashed down to the field. When she looked up at everyone staring at her, she wanted to disappear in a hole. Immediately the bleachers collapsed. Many children were hurt.'

Florence may have been right on this occasion but, wrote Joy, it brought her little happiness. 'This aunt of mine was a much misunderstood woman and had a sad life.'

Lesley Skeels, now a mother living in Berkshire, also

found it unpleasant to have a premonition — not because she was blamed for something that happened but because she was nicknamed 'Witchey-poo' at school. She and some friends had just got off the school bus one morning and were waiting at the kerb for the cars to pass so they could cross over to get to school. Two hundred yards down the road, a car turned out of a junction into the main road towards the school. Lesley turned to her friend Sylvie and said: 'I think that woman is going to run you over.'

The woman stopped the car and some of the children crossed over. She was shaking and there was something strange about her, says Lesley. Sylvie stepped off the kerb and Lesley tried to stop her, but the woman started up the car and ran Sylvie over. Fortunately Sylvie was only badly shaken and bruised.

Predictions need not always bring bad news but can sometimes herald a relatively minor event. Julie says that when her son was just starting to talk, at about nine o'clock one morning, he suddenly mentioned a Mrs Hansard.

'I was surprised because she was an old family friend whose name he would never have heard in his life. I had not spoken nor heard of her since I was a child. But that day, out of the blue, I got a letter from her.' Coincidence or something deeper? With the sometimes uncertain state of the mail it would be useful to have a child around the house who could accurately predict when letters were going to arrive — or even better, alert you when they got lost in the post.

Another Dorothy, who is a psychic artist and colour therapist, says that a predictive dream revealed the whereabouts of the grandfather she desperately wanted as a child.

'My one grandad died before I was born and my father's father was just not there. My father thought he was dead. One day when I was seven and a half, I got to my nan's house and the door was locked. I panicked because it was always open. She let us in and a gentleman was there.

'He gave my sister and I half a crown each for sweets and his ration book to take to the sweet shop. When we got back (we hadn't nearly been able to spend all that money on sweets — it was a fortune) Gran said: "Go down to the station and watch the trains while you are eating your sweets."

'When we got back from our feast, the man was gone. "Who was that?" I asked Gran.

' "Oh, that was your grandad," she said.

'So I did have a grandad like other children. But he was gone again.

'I started to dream about finding him. I used to see myself get out of the front door and through the garden. I tried going all sorts of ways out of Nottingham until eventually I found grandad's house. It was a very wide road, down a very steep hill that narrowed at the bottom. There was a railway track that went under the road. I stopped at the junction and one way the road passed some trees. There was grandfather living in a big house being looked after by servants. I had the dream for several years.

'My grandmother died when I was 25. In the following May my aunt contacted my mother to say that she had discovered where Grandad was.

'He had written to my grandmother sending money, but she had been in hospital for six months and her old house had been sold in that time. The old man had been in hospital himself and his address had changed. I arranged to go with my husband and children to see him the next day.

'We found ourselves in a very wide road. I said, "I can direct you", because it was all exactly as in the dream — the railway going under the road, the trees and even the big house where my grandfather was living. In a sense, the dream was totally accurate because grandad was being looked after by servants. They were care assistants. He was living in an old people's home.'

I found that children could apparently spark off premonitions as well as have them. Of Maureen's four children, Colin, the youngest, aged 17, was the only one still living at home. 'We were a loving, close-knit family, very talkative and enjoying each other's company. One night I had a dream. I dreamed that Colin was dead. I was standing in the kitchen, very distressed. I was saying: "Colin's dead and Myra [a friend of the family] doesn't even know." There seemed to be no body or the scene of death. He just wasn't around.

'I didn't even think of it when I first got up out of bed. It came back to me as dreams do when Colin was ready to leave to catch the school bus. I was standing by the kitchen sink when he came up and said: "I'm going now, mum."

'I replied, "Oh, Colin, I dreamed you were dead." I looked at him and he put his arms round my chest, as he was so much taller than I was and I hugged him close. He laughed and I put my hands up and brought his face down to mine to kiss him for sheer joy and love. He smiled his gentle, smirky smile when I said I was so glad he wasn't dead, that he always gave when he was pleased.

'This wasn't our usual morning farewell as we mostly were in a tearing rush to get out. I followed him to the door. He'd been eager to ask a particular girl out. I said: "There's plenty more fish in the sea if she says no."

'He laughed and went off to catch his bus.'

Maureen said that Colin's father who was retired and always stayed in bed until the family rush was over, had got up specially to watch Colin walk to the bus stop, thinking to himself what a fine young man his son had grown into.

Colin had little to do at school that afternoon and his family believe he came home early but just missed his father, mother and grandmother who had gone out for a short drive. They think he came home, found the door locked (he had left his key in his bedroom) and went for a walk down a nearby lane which leads to cliffs 200 feet high. He was not seen again for two days.

During that time, wrote Maureen, there were some odd occurrences. 'The following morning my mother was about to get up and was half awake so she could have been dreaming. She thought she saw Colin in a corner of the bedroom. He was leaning against a wall or rock with his coat half over his shoulder and his right eye cut and blood running down the side of his face.

'My mother said she put out her arms to him and said, "Colin, Colin, is that you Colin?" but he just faded away.

'During the day. I had a strong desire to go and look along the shore, though there was no more reason he should have gone there than anywhere else. The weather was atrocious, the wettest two days for many years. There was a thick dark mist. By tea-time, I felt so impelled to walk down the lane to the cliffs where there was an old mine shaft, I ploughed through the mist and on reaching the mine-shaft, called for Colin.

'We didn't know that he lay on the rocks below us. The edge where he had gone over and met his death was in direct line at the foot of which his body was found two days later, smashed on the rocks below.

'The following Tuesday, I was getting tea ready in the kitchen, when I had the oddest sensation again. My friend Myra, the Myra of the dream, was due home from her holiday abroad. She had not been told the bad news. I suddenly realised she was due home that day and said: "Myra is coming home today and she doesn't know that Colin is dead."

'It was like a replay of the dream. The evening before the funeral, my family arrived. There were 14 of us. I decided it would be best if I slept in Colin's bed. Such a feeling of love and peace I have never experienced either before or since. I felt cocooned in absolute peace as I lay in Colin's bed. I slept like a log.

'My eldest son told me I was just seeing into things what I wanted — perhaps he is right. I don't know but I sometimes feel as if all these incidents were a glimmer of something perhaps to comfort us. It seems strange that of all our family Colin was the one who was always afraid to go near the edges of cliffs. I once told my husband having children was "like holding a beautiful glass bauble that could so easily break".

'It's almost as if I had to say goodbye to him. Since then, there has been nothing.'

Marian wrote from Ireland: 'The first time I got a

premonition was when I was 15. I was sewing in school when I suddenly dropped the sewing. I got a terrible urge to go home. My father was very ill at home at the time and the ambulance was due to call for him at 5pm as he was going to Dublin. The nun asked me what was wrong. I told her I had to go home and I could not even wait to get permission from the Reverend Mother. I even left my school bag behind so I could run faster. When I ran in the door at home, my mother said: "How did you know?"

'It seems they got word that the ambulance had to come earlier and so I was there to see him off and I had a terrible feeling that he would never be back even though I had not been told at the time that he had cancer. I never saw my father again.'

Ellie too has many premonitions which come either as pictures in her mind or as feelings. When I met her she was 15 and told me: 'When I was about 12, I was sat watching the television at school when my mind went blank and I thought to myself, "If my father has had an accident I shall take him in hospital a small bunch of grapes with a huge red ribbon tied to them". About five minutes later there was a phone call from my mother, who was crying, to tell me that dad had had an accident and was in hospital.

'Last week I was constantly thinking about a family which we knew in America. In all my lessons I sat and thought about them and their boat, where they lived and their way of life. On the Saturday morning of that same week, I received a phone call from my father telling me they had been in a car crash. The husband and child were both dead but the wife had survived.'

Michelle's dream which predicted an accident for her

uncle when she was 15 was powerful enough to return three times. She wrote: 'I had a dream about my uncle. He was covered to the chin with a white sheet. He was very ill. I said, "What's the matter John?" but he could not tell me. The following night I had the dream again. I asked him if he had been in an accident but he could not answer and I woke up screaming.

'The third night I had the dream again. I told my mum the next morning. A month later at 5.30am I woke up with a terrific pain in my head. I fell back to sleep but an hour and a half later my mum woke me to say John had been in a car accident about an hour before. She went to see him in hospital. He was covered up to the chin with a massive white sheet (as in my dream).'

Memories of predictive dreams which have come true can stay vivid over the years. In 1932 Ronald was in his first year at secondary school. He shared art lessons with boys from other forms and greatly admired a boy called Peter, though he was too shy to speak to him.

'During the long summer holiday, I had a dream that I attended Peter's funeral and as I write, I can see the coffin being lowered into the grave, though I had never so far as I can recollect, attended a funeral. The impression was so vivid that as soon as school recommenced after the holiday, I asked after him of a form mate whom I knew lived near Peter. He told me that Peter had died from diptheria during the school holiday.'

James's mother did not take him seriously when, at the age of 13, he told her he had dreamt about a disaster. 'I had a dream about a big boat that left the harbour then went half way out then crashed and was lying on its side. In the morning, I told my mum and she said 'Don't worry, you dream about anything' and pulled my leg about it.

'I was really worried and wondered if I ought to phone the police, but I thought they would think it was a stunt or I was a crank. Then two days later there was the Zeebrugge disaster.'

Dreams about disasters are common and there are some well documented cases involving children. In April 1912, a 14-year-old girl in Nottingham told her grandmother about a dream in which a large boat kept sinking in the local park. The next day news broke of the sinking of the Titanic. The girl's uncle, the ship's engineer, was among the dead.

After the Aberfan disaster in 1966 when part of a giant coal tip slid down on to a village school in South Wales, killing 128 children and 16 adults, Dr J.C. Barker made a nationwide appeal for premonitions about the tragedy. In his book, *Scared to Death*, he records that one of the few accurate predictions, and certainly the saddest, came from the parents of a 10-year-old victim. Shortly before the disaster, she had told her mother that she had dreamed she had gone to school and there was no school there. Something black had come down all over it.

A problem with that study was that it asked about a past event. It is easy to say: 'Oh I knew that was going to happen,' afterwards. But unless you have told anyone your prediction in advance you may not be believed.

However, it might be best not to try to formalise children's predictive ability. How could you guard against children with such a priceless gift being exploited, either by greedy individuals or the state?

If we could isolate this ability, which would turn current scientific theories about time on their head, and then if we could develop it, there is no guarantee that all the gifted children we discovered would be willing to increase any power they might have. Such a gift might even frighten them.

May's 15-year-old daughter regularly knows when things are going to happen but the ability worries her. On one occasion, she woke afraid and weeping and said: 'If we get through Friday, we'll be all right.'

'We did get through Friday,' said May. 'Then I heard that a dear friend travelling in the USA had had a serious injury on Friday and had to be flown for surgery.

'My daughter often seems to know who is going to phone fifteen minutes before they do. She will say, "Don't get the coffee yet. Esther is going to ring you." There is usually no special time that the people concerned ring, so it is really strange. My daughter doesn't like this and is not keen to develop it.'

In the midst of all the questions of proof and research it's often forgotten that premonitions can be frightening for a young person and they do need reassurance that they are not responsible for the tragedy they couldn't prevent yet had knowledge of. For we are talking about real children and teenagers whose experiences can cause tremendous inner conflicts and questions. Berenice told me: 'When my father was about 12 he was walking along a country road near his home. He saw three men building a tall wall and heard a voice say quite clearly, "By tomorrow those three men will be dead".

'Dad didn't know what to do. He was afraid to speak out

in case the men were angry with him or that he might be wrong. But the next day he heard that the wall had collapsed and the three men had been killed. After that my father completely shut his mind to the psychic but found it hard to forgive himself for keeping silent.'

Real premonitions are rare and are very urgent and sudden, totally different in quality and intensity from normal anxieties. So a child issues a warning we should listen and maybe change our plans. Children can have many underlying anxieties especially over parents' safety and these can manifest themselves as pleas to be careful or not leave them. It may be a general anxiety about the stresses of life.

As a working mum I know how hard it is with all the dashing and last minute panics to say goodbye calmly and spend minutes reassuring little ones as the clock ticks away. But it is vital. And of course where a parent is concerned about work or travel the child may be picking up anxieties telepathically.

Anne Calandro who lives in Marietta in Georgia, in the United States, had this experience: 'Last summer I took a part-time job most of which I could do from home but which involved some driving to a city an hour away. I dislike interstate driving and always fear getting into an accident. I never voiced this in front of my youngest daughter who was then only three. Yet she said to me every time I left, "Please don't die today, Mommy".

'Before that time and afterwards she has never mentioned death or seemed the least perturbed when I leave her to go out for a while. It made me feel a little weird when she said it but I realise now she was not having a premonition but picking up on my own unspoken fears.'

But as with telepathy some premonitions can be quite routine if rather strange. Paul, who lives in Kent, is a very down-to-earth person and his eight-year-old son, Thomas, has shown few traces of being other-worldly. Yet two incidents have given Paul food for thought. The first was when Thomas was talking to his mother, Mandy, and suddenly asked: 'Do dogs bump into things?'

'No,' she explained, 'they're usually too well co-ordinated.'

Then she forgot about the question until later in the day when she was taking her dog round to her mother's house. As they walked in the dog was distracted by some movement outside, turned its head and walked into the door.

A coincidence? A one-off? Paul thought it was unusual at the time but months later when he had taken his family to London, Thomas asked him, apparently for no reason: 'Have you ever been in a car crash, Dad?'

Paul told him about a minor accident he had been in and Thomas seemed satisfied. He had to stay in London and work so his family went home without him. Later that evening Mandy rang Paul to say that the taxi which had taken them home from the station had been in a slight accident but they were uninjured.

Now Paul is wondering what else Thomas is going to come out with.

Perhaps young children have no sense of the limitations of time and are not aware they shouldn't know things in advance. Carla Randall who lives in Leeds told me: 'When my daughter Rhiannon was three she was sitting in the bike seat. We were going to visit a woman she hadn't met before. But Rhiannon insisted over and over again, "We're going to see the duck."

' "No, there are aren't any ducks on the way, Rhiannon," I told her."

'But she insisted: "The lady's duck, mummy. She's got a duck at her house."

'I didn't bother to argue though I knew she wouldn't have. When we got there however the woman had got a porcelain duck on the living room wall. "There you are, Rhiannon," I said, "your duck."

'But Rhiannon wasn't satisfied. "Not that sort of duck, mummy, a real one."

' "Oh," interrupted the woman, "she's right. We used to have a real duck. He swam on the pond in the garden till he got eaten by a fox last year".'

Chapter Five

Ghosts

IF A CHILD does see a ghost it is often hard for him or her to confide in sceptical adults. Vivien Greene, widow of the writer Graham Greene, told me that she saw one when she was six. 'My father, Sidney B. Browning, was a manager in the British American Tobacco Company. It meant that my family, my mother, myself and my younger brother were always being moved from place to place and even when very small I hated these constant moves.

'My father spent some time in Munich but we did not follow him there and at Long Ashton near Bristol, twice to Liverpool, then Nailsea and at one time to Antwerp where I think we lived for a year.

'It was in winter probably December one evening and I was standing in front of the stairs.

'The staircase was on my left, a narrow passage ran

down in front of me to what I think was the back door; a sitting room door was on my right. Suddenly the door and the wall at the end of the passage disappeared and I saw the dark blue night sky with glittering stars in the winter sky. Between me and the air, but nearer where the door had been, stood a child of about my own age, naked, perfectly solid in appearance and colour with the extraordinary addition, in which I was much interested and noticed more than anything else, of white silk openwork socks, what I thought of as party socks.

'We looked at each other and my mother called out from the sitting room, "Finn, there's a terrible draught. Do shut the door", or words to that effect, whether in French — Finn was the cook — or English I do not know. Instantly the apparition vanished and the wall and the door were as normal. I did not speak of this for at least ten years and felt even then very reluctant to mention it. It was a rather sacred and holy experience and I still think of it with much awe and wonder.

'The date would have been 1910 or 1911 as I remember being taken to a window to see Bleriot's plane in the sky.'

Vivien did not discover the identity of her apparition. Often children see the ghosts of friends or family. Grandparents are a favourite and in a later chapter I tell how they often assume the role of guardian angel to their grandchildren. But occasionally they just pop in with a message for the adults who can't see them so easily.

Pam who lives in Devizes told me: 'When I was five months pregnant with my son I lost my dad. When my son was a toddler and able to talk I left him with my mum one day while I went shopping. When I got back my mum was very upset. Apparently Neil had been playing with his toys on the floor when he suddenly stopped and looked at a corner of the room as if he was annoyed at being called, went over to nothing, took nothing and trotted over to his nan and said, "I've got some flowers for you".

'Thinking it was a game my mum said, "Thank you. They are lovely."

'"Oh. They're not from me," Neil replied, "they're from him". Neil trotted over to a row of family pictures and picked out one of his grandad. Everyone was very upset at the time but afterwards we were all very comforted to think that Dad was still around.'

Chloe was ten and at boarding school in Torbay. Her bosom friend was Carla and the girls had sworn undying friendship as many pre-teenage girls do. One weekend Carla had gone out with an aunt for the day and Chloe wasn't expecting her friend back till late. It was dark when Chloe woke up to find her friend standing by her bed in her cubicle. 'Get away from my bed, Carla,' Chloe said crossly. 'Stop mucking about, I'm tired.' Chloe turned over and went back to sleep.

When she woke the next morning, Chloe went to her friend's cubicle to ask about her day out. But her friend's bed hadn't been slept in and straight away Chloe knew her friend had died. At that moment the housemistress came in to break the news to Chloe that her friend had been killed in an accident with a swing in a park playground late the previous afternoon.

'But there was no need to tell me,' Chloe said. 'We always promised each other that if one of us died the other would come back to say goodbye.'

Matthew, who lives in Berkshire, is an only child, very bright and very articulate. His mother, Veronica, told me that when Matthew was about two, he used to be taken every Saturday to an old people's home to see his great-grandmother who was suffering from progressive senile dementia. She became incapable of speech and her eyesight became very poor.

Towards the end, the only person she would respond to was Matthew. Veronica and his father would take him in front of the old lady and place his hands on the metal tray beside her bed. It was a routine they had. Matthew's dad would tap on the tray to attract her attention. Then she would run her fingers over Matthew's face, smile and try to make noises.

Veronica says that Matthew treated her as if she was another child. He called her his 'little great-nanny' as she had shrunk to around four foot in height and was very frail. When she died, Matthew was not three. He was taken to her funeral because he did not take well to being left with other people and, as he did not really know what was going on, Veronica was confident he would not be upset.

Nor was he. 'Matthew had his head lifted towards the crematorium ceiling which was totally plain,' she said. 'As the coffin came along, he started to say he could see his great-nanna on the ceiling. "Look there's little great-nanny. She's smiling," he kept saying looking upwards. He carried on saying this until the curtains closed around the coffin. "Look, she's gone now," he said. There was no mistaking what Matthew said because he was so articulate.

'Matthew saw his little great-nanny a couple of times in

his bedroom over the next couple of months, though not on the night of the funeral. He would say nanna or little great-nanny is smiling. He wasn't at all frightened. He is now six and he hasn't mentioned seeing her since.'

Young children will try to make sense of death in terms of their limited experience and vivid imaginations. Had Matthew picked up someone other than his parents saying 'She's gone above' and used that to try to make sense of why great-nanny had disappeared? Did he think as he could not go to see nanna any more, she might come to him. Children do work hard at making sense of death.

George Wall, a professor of philosophy at Lamar University in Texas, thinks that psychological explanations are not always adequate for a child's spiritual experiences. In Matthew's case, it is hard to explain the crematorium incident away. Perhaps his grandmother did continue to smile with the only person she had communicated with to the end, the only person who could still make her smile.

Grandad Bert was a family member who perhaps thought he had better alert everyone that he had passed over, or attendance would be a bit thin on the ground at the funeral, as he was not the world's most popular character. Which is perhaps why he appeared to the youngest member of the family, whom he might have thought would give him the most enthusiastic reception. It was left to his young great-granddaughter, who was only 21-months-old, to alert her family to his demise.

Carla told me that she and the children hardly ever saw Grandad Bert. He was an overbearing man at the best of times and when he developed senile dementia, became so problematic that Carla could not face taking the children to see him.

He died unexpectedly at about 4am on a Wednesday morning, but since the family had lost touch, Carla was not told about the death.

'At about 11 in the morning,' said Carla, 'Layla stopped playing in the living room and looked up as if she was looking into someone's face. "It's grandad Bert," she said and she ran to where, apparently, he was standing, looked up into his face and then shrugged as if to say, "Oh he's gone". Then she ran back and carried on playing.

'I thought this was odd as we never saw Grandad Bert. So when my husband came home about 4pm I said: "I suppose we'd better see if he's all right". So he rang his mum and she said that grandad Bert had died early that morning.'

Did the ghost that no one particularly wanted to see decide to appear to someone who was most likely to be most co-operative and tip off the family?

In Julie's case, she wasn't the only person to see her late uncle. But Aunty Doris, his widow, who chatted to him regularly was regarded as a bit dotty by the rest of the family. When she was five or six, Julie, would go on family visits to the aunt which were regarded as a bit of a chore.

'When we went round,' said Julie, 'there she was chatting away to her dead husband. They thought she was off her trolley, but I could see him as well. Aunty took me into the bedroom to give me a sweet. She said: "You don't think I'm dotty, do you? You can see him".

'I had never met him in real life, but from pictures, I

realised it was him I saw. I did not say anything to anybody (I don't know why).'

If someone who is loved and cared for by the family dies, why should his spirit fly round the world to someone he has barely seen to bring news of his departure from this life? Mandy, then aged 13, was living in Perth, Australia, when her great uncle died in England. Though he had suffered from lung cancer, he had been ill for a relatively short time and Mandy's family had not been told about it. But when Mandy's great-aunt rang to tell them her husband had died, Mandy's dad was already making plans to come to England to help.

The previous night, Uncle Fred had appeared to Mandy at the end of her bed. She came into her parents' room crying: 'Uncle Fred's dead. I saw him.'

However, Mandy had never met Uncle Fred and had not been to England since she was five, when Fred had in fact been visiting Australia. She had seen no recent photos of Uncle Fred, yet recognised him instantly.

The story of the apparition caused some trouble in the family as Fred had a 15-year-old daughter who had helped to nurse him. She and her sisters were upset that he had not appeared to them, but to a comparative stranger halfway around the world.

Thomas tells the story of his mother who when a young girl met her gran in the street. 'She was walking with her four sisters and saw her granny coming towards them and stepped off the footpath to let her go by. Gran did not speak as she seemed wrapped up in her thoughts.

'Mum's sister said, "What did you do that for? There's no one there." Mother said nothing. She saw her gran complete with poke bonnet and shawl, but her sisters had seen nothing. When she got home, her mother told them that gran had died.'

But a prize for the most unconventional return would have to go to Jane's grandmother who apparently performed an act of supernatural ventriloquism. When Jane's daughter was four-and-a-half, the family were staying in Aberdeen for a christening.

'The eldest child of the family we were staying with was being a real pain, so I took him and my daughter to the local park. We were playing in the bandstand in the twilight, dancing round to Ring-a-roses. We got to a bit I didn't know about "fishes in the water, fishes in the sea". We were skipping round when my daughter's voice changed and she was singing in the voice of my much loved paternal grandma who had been dead for twelve years. She had her funny accent —- a Welsh one — and was emphasising the words exactly as nan used to. I expected to see my nan there. It was a very happy experience. I think I had been thinking about all the times my nan had taken me to the park when I was a child and the happy times we had.'

Sheila's grandson was born about five months after his father, Kevin, died in a car accident. Darren is now eleven and although he never knew his father, follows his dad in every way: the same looks, the same mannerisms and the same love of football.

'He walks like his dad, talks like his dad, writes like his dad,' says Sheila. However, he has been brought up in an area well away from his former home as his grief-stricken mother, Debbie, who was widowed at 21, could bear no reminders of Kevin.

But, according to Sheila, Kevin has been part of Darren's life since he was very young. She says that when he was six he told her: 'I see my daddy Kevin. I know my daddy Kevin, I love my daddy Kevin, but it is so difficult to talk to adults about it. But you know, nanny, you understand.

Sheila remembers: 'When Darren was only two-and-a-half, we were living in a country cottage and he was staying with us and his mum. Suddenly he pointed over to a chair and said, "Look, mummy, there's the nice daddy man." He was pointing to Kevin's special chair.

'Debbie asked him: "Where? What are you talking about?"

' "It's the daddy man in our picture," Darren explained. "Oh, he's gone now." '

When Darren was three, Sheila got out some old photos to amuse him. 'One showed Kevin with a group of friends when he was eight. I had to stand and think which one was my son,' she told me, 'but Darren identified his father straight away. "Look Nan," he cried, "Boy Kevin, boy daddy".'

But his mother was very upset by the incident, saying: 'Oh, no, not that again, he keeps on and on that he sees his daddy and talks to him.'

Darren at eleven, says Sheila, still continues to see and talk to his father, though he loves his stepfather and his new brother very much and is very happy in his new life. But Daddy Kevin is still there for him.

Sally told me that she also kept hearing the phantom voice of her father for the first four months after he died when she was 13. 'It was typical of him,' she said. 'He came in the door and shouted. "Ooo-ooh" as he used to when he was alive. Once mum and I heard him at the same time. I was upstairs and I heard him call downstairs and she was downstairs and heard him calling upstairs. I once heard him when I was taking the dog out for a walk. Another time, I was sitting at the dining room table doing my homework. As I looked up, he was on the stairs holding the banisters. He was wearing clothes I recognised, but as I looked at his face, he vanished. I wasn't scared, It was nice, I just thought, "It's dad but it can't be". Although I never saw him again, I used to feel him around.'

Sue who was eight passed her dad on the stairs one evening. He was wearing his coat and scarf. 'Hello, Dad,' she said, 'where are you off to?'

'To take my things upstairs of course,' he replied.

It seemed so ordinary that it was a shock when she remembered he'd been dead for two weeks. She turned round and he was gone.

Three-year-old Kenny who lived in Bournemouth didn't even know his Great-Uncle Clancy in Ireland but one afternoon he said to his Nan: 'I've just seen Clan-Clan. He came to tell me he's dead but he's all right.' Clan-Clan was Uncle Clancy's pet name that had been used when he was a child by their mum. Kenny's gran who told me the story, said that her brother had been ill for some time but there hadn't been any recent news as the family wasn't in close touch. Soon after the message came of Clancy's death.

A couple of years later Kenny stopped and looked and said 'Oh Clan-Clan' but would say no more.

Sometimes the appearance of a dead father or grandfather can cause problems especially if he comes back to a child with a message we can't understand. Janice told me that her husband had died not long before her daughter was born: 'When I was in labour I knew that I was having a little girl and I could feel my dead husband by my side holding my hand. My sister who was with me knew he was there too. When my daughter was about two-and-a-half I went out for the evening with my new boyfriend leaving my sister babysitting. During the evening I received a frantic phone call to come home. When I got there my future mother-in-law was there as well as my sister had phoned her. My sister had gone into Sian's bedroom earlier in the evening as she had heard her laughing. Sian was sitting up in bed talking to someone and laughing. "Who are you talking to?" my sister asked her.

' "That nice man there by the window. He comes to see me and reads me stories."

'Then Sian broke off and spoke to whoever she could see. "No, you mustn't do that," she said. "The other man's telling the nice man off," she explained to my sister.

'At that point my sister had dragged Sian out of the bedroom and phoned me and my mother-in-law. Then my bedroom door started banging — it takes two of us to move it as it is stuck —a nd the banging continued till my footsteps were heard.

'I had a chat with my daughter and she told me, "That man I chat to. He's nice and he often comes. The other man told him off and said the papers are in the bank."

'I showed Sian various photos of men in our family and she picked out my husband as the nice man and my grandad who had died the year before as the man who had told him off. We moved soon after my husband died. But we can't work out what the papers in the bank are. Sian wouldn't have her window open after that in case the man came back and doesn't mention the man now.'

It's hard to tell whether Sian became afraid of the man because the adults got so upset but the mystery of the papers remains unsolved. Perhaps I'll be able to give the answer in another book.

Skipper was in his early eighties but had a special soft spot for the small boys in his Boys Brigade troop especially for James a boisterous six-year-old with an eye for mischief. To the amazement of James's parents, Skipper kept James to a 60-minute sponsored silence (55-minutes anyway) to help a local charity.

Skipper made a proud sight laying his wreath at the local War Memorial on Remembrance Day and James stood straight and silent with the other lads through the long ceremony under Skipper's eagle but loving eye.

Just after Christmas Skipper died suddenly and totally unexpectedly after a minor operation. James didn't say much but a few days later he got up in the morning and told his mother: 'I had a lovely dream about Skipper last night. He was young and really well and had his little dog with him. The dog was running after a ball and Skipper was chasing him through the fields and the flowers. I wanted to play but Skipper said he had to go but I must try to help mum and "Well done, James".'

Skipper's dog who was old and blind and had accompanied his master everywhere, was put to sleep very shortly after James' dream.

Other ghosts are not related at all to the people who see

them, although there may be a strong emotional link. In the case of Genevie who lived near San Diego, California, it was the child who was the ghost.

Genevie's cousin Joy told me the story. 'Genevie was substitute teaching in a school near San Diego in the 1970s. One little boy in her class was very sensitive, abysmally poor and very much in need of attention. He was Mexican. Genevie liked him very much and did what she could for him.

'One Saturday, as she drove along the main road, the little boy jumped smiling right in front of her car. She was so startled she swerved and sat at the road side recovering. But she couldn't see the little boy anywhere. The family had no phone and doubled up in a shack some place and she couldn't find out if he was all right until the Monday morning. Then she received notice that he was drowned at the very moment she saw him. She feels he came to say goodbye to her.'

Patricia told me that when she was 12, she saw the ghost of a woman with a big shawl, a Spanish comb in her hair and rings on her fingers. She was about 75. 'I was very scared when I saw her and she vanished when I spoke. I told mum, but she told me not to be silly and to go back to bed. I had six brothers and sisters and must not frighten them.'

Pat was listening on the stairs and heard her mum say to her dad, 'Pat's just seen Old Mother Moore'. This was the woman who had died while living in the shop which Pat's parents had taken over.

Wendy's ghosts weren't even the conventional 'lady in grey' type though in their own way just as exotic. 'When

I was about four,' she told me, 'We lived in Derby by the prison. My dad worked on the railway. I woke up one night to see two figures on the end of my bed boxing. They were two men dressed as boxers, with long boxing shorts. They were full-sized.

'There was an old army blanket at the window to dim the light from the street lamp but I saw them very clearly and was unafraid. I was quite awake and very curious.

'I didn't mention the incident to my parents. I didn't want to be told off for being silly. I did tell another child who used to walk me home from school. She told me very firmly that there were no ghosts but the Holy Ghost. I think I made an early decision that God's disapproval was too much of a risk. I don't remember ever seeing another ghost.'

As a child, Jane, now in her thirties, twice saw people no one else could see. The first time was when she was 10 or 11 and attending a school swimming gala at an old Edwardian baths. Throughout the proceedings, a strange little girl kept coming in and out of the gallery opposite, with a little wooden sword, a pinny with a red cross on and strange clothes made of crepe paper.

'I found it most distracting. Yet no one else seemed to notice. Afterwards when I asked, I was the only person to see her.

'Not long after I was on a school visit and passed a big old house on a trip up to London. It was a white building and the garden was absolutely filled with people in old style peasant costume, picking fruit on the trees. When I asked, discreetly, no one else had seen anything. When I went past the house years later, the garden was very small, nothing like the orchard I had seen.'

In Beverley's case, her mother also saw the ghosts, though it was not till many years later that she admitted it. Beverley remembers: 'I woke in the middle of the night to find several human figures floating past the bed. The figures were like sharp shadows, black in silhouette, but not against a wall — rather like black cardboard cut-outs in profile. There were several, but I was most aware of a portly gentleman who passed by. The image was so sharp that I can recall the outline of the waistcoat buttons and cutaway coats.

'As they went out of the door, I seemed to lose sight of them. I called out to my mother who came into the room. She didn't acknowledge them at the time. She later told me she hadn't wanted to frighten me. I remember saying, "One's just gone right through you".'

At the time, Beverley lived very close to a traditionally Quaker area and in later life has been drawn towards Quakerism, though she has not become a member.

Beverley's mother, Joy, does recall the incident and says that her motive for telling Beverley at the time that she was dreaming was that she did not want to worry her. 'I remember it very clearly. I wish I had written the date down in my diary but at the time was more anxious to gloss the incident over although strangely it was not at all frightening.

'But I thought at the time, Beverley might have been worried. On this particular night, she called out and I got out of bed and went to her bedroom which was next to ours. On reaching the door, I was startled to see these groups of figures standing just inside the door.

'As Beverley said, they were a small group of dark figures, very plain but the faces were not clear. They appeared to be wearing cloaks and had tall hats which led us to believe they might be Quakers.

'I moved forward and suddenly they glided towards the end of the room and disappeared. We did both notice one of the figures was shorter than the others.'

Childhood ghosts are often remembered vividly many years later. They stand out as different from fantasies and dreams. 'It was neither reality nor dreaming,' was how Wendy described her experience. While many memories are changed by subsequent experience, particularly vivid episodes can be preserved intact.

A non-psychic example comes from the 'flashbulb' memories that seem to take in the surrounding context. People can often remember what they were doing the day John Kennedy was assassinated or when men first walked on the moon. The music they were listening to, what they were wearing, who they were with — these trivial details seem to have stuck to the moment.

Some children seem to pick up things, apparently from another world that, when checked out, prove to be true and beyond the child's current knowledge.

Madame Robert now lives in Brittany in a home full of treasures from Pondicherry, the French enclave in India where she and her sister were brought up before the second world war. Her sister, Denise, appears to have been highly sensitive to psychic phenomena.

Their father held an important post in the district and often the village headmen would come to see him in his garden to discuss business. Denise was eight when she said to her father one evening: 'There's the old head of the village who has a hole in his ear. He's come and he says he wants to see you.'

'We searched everywhere,' recalled Madame Robert, 'but there was no one. The next day, the son of the village head came in the morning and announced to my father that the chief had died the previous evening at the time Denise had said she had seen him.'

Some years later Madame Robert bought a property at on the outskirts of Pondicherry. It was near a lake and dated back to 1800. She, her mother and teenage sister had gone for a moonlight picnic at the lake. Suddenly Denise said: 'I see something beside the tree. It's a woman all clothed in white who is holding something in her hands and is crying. Behind her is a man dressed in a large checked cape and he has a beard.'

'My mother who was very interested by all matters of this sort said to Denise: "Ask her what her name is." My sister asked several times and told us that the woman was called Theresa.

'We did not find out why she was crying.

'The next day I went to see the man who sold me the property and asked if they still had the documents from the time the house was built. He produced a huge packet of documents and we found that the house had belonged to Mme Theresa de Colomb.

'My sister often saw the lady in white but we could never learn why she was crying.

'Eventually, because it is not healthy to cohabit with phantoms we asked a priest to purify the area. This was done.

'Two other people who learned I had bought the property came to tell me of visions they had had. One spoke of the woman in white who cried and the other of the man with the beard and checked cape. However, we did not talk about Denise's visions.'

Sometimes a child can see a ghost in a particular place when he is too young to know of the local legend. In the case of Old Mother Dyer it was slightly more complicated.

Joan Jefferies of Swindon told me: ' I often go and talk to different groups in the area and one evening an elderly gentleman got up and said he lived in a small village just outside Swindon. When he was a small boy he had been playing hide and seek with his friends. He was standing by a gate hiding his eyes with his hands while he counted to a hundred.

'To his amazement when he looked up there was an old lady standing on the other side of the gate looking at him. She had a long black cloak and a black poke bonnet and was pushing a huge black pram with a baby in it. He was absolutely terrified and abandoning his game ran home to tell his mother.

She said he was just being silly but nevertheless she mentioned his experience to an elderly neighbour who didn't laugh but told her, "Oh your lad saw Old Mother Dyer who used to take unwanted babies away and put them in freshly dug-open graves while they were still alive. She was hanged in 1896 and has been seen in that spot many times by young children since her death".'

Fascinated I mentioned Joan's story to Pat, a friend of mine who lives in Reading and was surprised at her reaction. 'Oh no, Mother Dyer belongs to Reading. When

I was a kid our mothers would threaten us that if we were naughty old Mother Dyer who was a baby farmer, would put us in the Clappers (the rapids in the Thames) at Caversham where she used to dump the babies. Some children saw her ghost.'

A bit of research uncovered that Amelia Dyer as she was called had moved in 1895 to Reading from Bristol where she had taken in unwanted children. Once in Reading, she began to advertise once more that she would foster and adopt children whose parents couldn't keep them.

It seems she would murder the children and dump their bodies in parcels or cases into the Thames while continuing to claim boarding fees from the parents. In April 1896 she was arrested and charged with the murder of seven infants though since she had been baby farming for fifteen years it was suspected that many more of her charges had met a similar fate.

She was executed in June, 1896 at Newgate and her ghost was reputed to haunt the chief warder.

So had she stopped on her way from Bristol to Reading and lived in Swindon for a while? As with all good legends we shall never know.

The real problem when children see ghosts, especially if no one is around at the time, is to be sure what it is the child is actually describing. Young children's language can be very vivid, but nevertheless, misleading. For example, we were camping in the New Forest last year when Jack came dashing into the tent and announced, 'Quick, mummy, there's an enormous panda bear outside.' Knowing we were less than 10 miles from Marwell Zoo Park, my first reaction was to panic and warn all and sundry that there was a wild animal loose.

My second instinct was to go back to sleep and assume it was a flight of Jack's fantasy world. Both reactions would have been wrong. When I looked out of the tent the panda turned out to be a large black and white cow, with a face marked just like the panda in Jack's story book. Jack had neither lied nor fantasised but, not having seen an animal like this before, he had described it in terms of his limited experience.

So the next time your child tells you: 'There's a ghost outside,' have a look. He might have got it completely wrong but on the other hand . . .

Chapter Six

Lives Cut Short

THE MOST HARROWING ghost stories I have been told were not tales of dreadful spectres armed with an array of Hollywood special effects. They were simple stories of ghosts of children.

Too often psychic investigators can forget that ghosts were once real flesh and blood people who lived and loved and were loved in return. When a child dies the death leaves a permanent scar on the souls of its parents. As the child psychiatrist, Janet Boucher, put it, although the mother may be physically separated from the baby when it is born, the links remain and when the child dies, emotionally a bit of the parent dies too.

When a handicapped child dies, the grief is not only for the child who died, but also for the child who never was. Jackie who died when she was 12 had never been able to speak or walk. Her mother told how her daughter died after a year in hospital and during that time the family had moved house so Jackie had never seen her new home. 'As I stood in the kitchen after the funeral, with my friends and family all round, above the chattering, I heard a voice. It said, "Don't worry about me, mummy. I am all right now."

'Jackie had never been able to speak, so she had never even said mummy. I have since wondered if I had wanted to hear that. On the other hand, I am sure I would have never expected her to talk. Jackie died before Christmas. On New Year's Eve, some friends came to stay the night with their young son who was about two-and-a-half years old. He slept with our three-year-old son.

'Some months later my friend told me what her son had said the following morning. She had not told me at the time for fear of upsetting me so soon after Jackie's death. He had asked her who was the little girl who had crossed the landing and looked into his bedroom. "You mean Christine [Jackie's younger sister]," his mother had said.

'But the little boy said, no, this little girl had white [blonde] curly hair. He had not seen Jackie since he was nine months old. Jackie could not walk either, even with help.'

Richard is a farmer in New Zealand who I met when he was visiting family in England. Sitting in the garden of a friend's house on a summer's day while his adopted son played with my children, he told me how an apparition had helped him come to terms with two tragedies.

His second son died when he was just a few days old at a time when the family were living in Rhodesia before it became Zimbabwe. The sanctions imposed against the country during the struggle for independence meant that Richard could not get the drugs to save the baby whose lungs were not fully developed.

Eleven years later, in New Zealand, Joseph, Richard's eldest son died. 'We had only known for about ten days that there was something very seriously wrong,' he said, 'though no one knew what. Joseph had spasms during which he appeared to have difficulty breathing. We thought he was just exhausted, the problem would pass and he would be fine again. On one occasion, the problem didn't pass and we took him to see a lady doctor who thought he had asthma attacks.

'Joseph got up one morning, late for him as he had been reading late in bed the night before. He came into the sitting room and I gave him some tea. I always made tea for the children when they got up. Joseph said he was not feeling well. "Where are you feeling ill?" I asked him. He had not been able to explain what was wrong before. For the first time, he pointed to his throat.

'Then he started to have spasms and lose control of his arms. I thought he was having an asthma attack. I brought him to the table, sat him down and put him in the position the doctor had shown me. "I'm going to die, dad," he said.

'I held his shoulders and the tops of his arms. He threw his arms and head back and went mauve. He was unable to breathe. I put him on the ground and began mouth to mouth resuscitation.

'I continued until a nurse arrived about 20 minutes later. The lady doctor arrived about 30 minutes after that. After the best part of an hour, she said, "We have to stop now. There is no hope of reviving him." The autopsy found he was suffering from a very rare form of throat cancer that had developed only within the previous three months. There had only been 17 cases of it in medical history in the whole of New Zealand. How on earth it could happen to my boy? Two days before he died, Joseph had sat on my lap. I put my arms round him and he said, "You're the best dad in the world I could have had."

'Looking back, it was almost as if he had experienced his life and was looking back, not as if he was going on, almost as if he knew he was going to die.'

Three years after Joseph's death, Richard was by himself in church on a Saturday evening after mass. 'I saw the two boys, but they were not the ages they were when they died. [The baby who died would have been a year younger than Joseph.] They were both in their teens, the ages they would have been if they had lived. Both the boys were wearing the uniform of a Catholic college in Wellington.

'Joseph, for reasons of his own, had great ambitions to attend the school when he was old enough. They were kneeling beside me.

'Nothing was said. It was extraordinary and affirmed to me that death is a mere episode with no final division. The spirit had continued to go on through the days for those boys.'

The psychologist, Dr Michael Jackson, says he has observed in a number of accounts that when people lose a child and see him several years later, he will often have grown by the right number of years.

A few months after meeting Richard, by lucky chance

I met his wife Helen, during her short trip to England. Unlike her husband, she had not seen the ghost of her son, Joseph, but she had heard from him. Not long after his death his best friend, Daniel, a boy of the same age, came to see her.

'I hope you don't mind me coming,' he said, 'but I saw Joe last night. Well, I didn't actually see him but I sort of felt him and I sort of heard him. I knew it was him because of his gravelly voice.' Helen says everyone thought Joe's voice was breaking. They did not realise that the harsh quality was one of the effects of his throat cancer.

Daniel told her: ' "Hello Dan," he said.

" 'Oh hello, Joe,' I said. "What do you want?"

' "Would you do something for me Dan?"

' "Yes Joe, what is it?"

' "Would you go and see mum for me."

' 'Yes Joe. What do you want me to tell her?"

' "Nothing. I just wanted you to see if she was all right." '

The second message came early in the new year from her friend Harriet who had attended a spiritualist meeting out of curiosity. She was bored stiff during the seance until suddenly the medium said 'I've got a 12-year-old boy here.' He clutched his throat. 'The boy died from throat cancer. The boy's mum's not here but her friend is.'

He came and stood by Harriet. 'Can you give his mum a message and tell her it's time she stopped grieving.'

Helen says the contact was comforting and soothing and wonderful.

It may be that the ghosts of children find contact and

comfort on the other side. Peter King of the Reading National Spiritualist Church says that when a child dies, his grandparents will often bring him up on the other side. Annette, an American, lost her four-year-old son during the Second World War. Afterwards she was very ill with chest pains. 'A month after he died, I had a dream. My mother who had died some years before was standing at the door. I hugged her and said, "What are you doing here?"

' "I've come because I had to see you," she replied. We went through into the kitchen and she picked up some bread and put it in the toaster.

'When it was ready, she buttered it and went to give it to me. "No," I said, "give it to the baby." My little boy was sitting in his high chair, looking very happy. "Now that's what I came for," said my mother. "Stop worrying about him. He's being well taken care of. He's a lovely little boy." When I woke up, the sun was streaming on my bed and my pains were gone.'

Flora's granddaughter died when she was 13 months old. 'I just couldn't believe she had gone and I would not settle down at night without thinking about her. I used to cry every night thinking about her because she was such a wonderful baby, though she must have been in a lot of pain.

'Then one night I felt a strange sensation and all of a sudden I was watching over my little granddaughter. She was happy and being looked after by my own mother. After seeing the baby so happy and out of pain, it really helped me. I told my daughter, who was the baby's mother, and it helped her too. She was a Down's syndrome baby, but was beautiful and gave plenty of love when she was with us.'

But what happens if the dead child is not greeted by people he knows on the other side? John, a father of three in Berkshire, who works for an airline, believes that, sometimes, drumming it into children's minds that they should not go off with strangers, can have unexpected results. For if a ghost child cannot find a friend he recognises in the afterlife, he may try to return to his mother. And if she is not there, then the other thing he has been taught to do is to go to the people over the road he has known all his short life.

He believes this is what happened to Paul, a neighbour's 10-year-old son, who was playing in a tin hut on a building site which caught fire. Paul suffered horrific burns and died in hospital five days later. Paul's mother, distraught with grief, moved out of her flat and refused to return to the area.

'My wife was so upset when she heard the news of Paul's death that she shut herself in the bathroom,' John told me. 'I was downstairs when suddenly Paul walked in through the front door but turned his back on me.'

'Weren't you upset when you saw Paul?' I asked. John said he simply reacted like many fathers would have done. 'Well I couldn't bear the thought of him wandering around with no one to talk to.

'I said: "Paul, won't you talk to me?" I couldn't see his face but I recognised his clothes. When I asked his mum later she said they were the ones he had worn on the day of the fire. Then I heard someone call his name.

' "Paul," I said, "You know you're always welcome

here, but I think some people want you to go with them.
I know you've been told not to go with people you don't
know but you must go with these people." I couldn't see
anyone else but I knew they were there.

'Then he was gone.

'I didn't say anything about seeing Paul because I
didn't want to upset my family. When my daughter, who
is only four, woke up I heard her call my eldest boy, who
is Paul's age. "Alec, I saw Paul last night," she told her
brother. Alec had been very close to Paul and was very
upset. "Don't be stupid, he's dead," he said.

' "I know he's dead," Samantha replied, "but he came
to my bedroom and said he was going to heaven and he
had come to say goodbye." She told her brother she had
seen his hands and face were burned and said she would
kiss them better. But he had told her, "Don't worry, I'll
be better soon."

'About six weeks later I went to a spiritualist church
some ten miles away from my home. The medium, Kitty,
said there was someone present who had helped a boy who
had been burned to death. I was still pretty upset about it
all and didn't really want to know but my friend nudged
me.

'The medium described how I had seen Paul and even
what my daughter had said. I had not told anyone what
had happened and had begun to wonder if it was all my
imagination but this was proof to me.

'I have seen Paul since at a different spiritualist church.
I had been on shift work and was pretty tired. The
medium was quite good but I was wishing I hadn't gone.
Then I saw Paul standing by me. I said to myself: "I'll

only believe this if the medium says something." Paul began talking to me and the medium said: "You've got a blonde boy standing next to you."

'I said, "It's OK, I've got the message." One of the things he asked me was to tell his mum he was OK now. The strange thing was that he was standing there with no clothes on with a friend of mine who'd died ten years ago and they were laughing at my puzzlement.

'Paul's body had been almost completely destroyed by the fire, even the soles of his feet. When I saw him, there wasn't a mark on his body. That's what he wanted me to tell his mum.'

It's not only children who see young ghosts. Some adults perhaps those who are especially sympathetic to children in this life seem to be open to the presence of ghostly children. Both David and his mother saw the child ghosts playing round the car.

David told me during a radio phone-in programme I was appearing on in the West Country: 'When I was 12 my parents took me to a very old pub. In the car park my mum suddenly said, "Look at those two girls."

'To my surprise I could see two little girls in crinoline-type dresses playing on the swings. Mum commented, "What sort of parents would leave children out playing on their own after dark?"

'By the time she'd undone her seat belt and we'd opened the car door the children were gone. There were fir trees and a heavy fence on one side and the girls hadn't come past the car which was the only other way out. What is more the swings were perfectly still.

'Later I discovered that about 150 years before a

cottage just down the road had been struck by a bolt of lightning and two young girls had been killed. I don't know if there was any connection but mum and I definitely saw those children.'

Another David, David Bryan, who lives in Hockley, Birmingham, told me: 'My wife Linda and I were going home one night when I saw about a dozen children playing in the street. Some were skipping, some playing hopscotch and others just sitting on the edge of the gutter. To my amazement my wife walked straight through them to cross the road and when I looked again they were gone. My wife had seen nothing.

'A couple of months later we were again going home, this time about 11pm and as I unlocked the car and got in a crowd of children appeared as if from nowhere and started dancing round the car. Linda asked me what I was waiting for and at that moment they disappeared.'

David Addis is a journalist and his child ghosts were a bit more upmarket. He was touring Bramshill Police College in Berkshire that had been the home of the Cope family for generations. Joan Cope's story is told in the last chapter of the book. David recalled: 'I went into a virtually empty room and I sensed the presence of two children who had been locked in there not through evil intent but to protect them from some sort of plague that had swept the house. Everyone else had died and they had perished but there was not a sad atmosphere because the children had been loved.'

I made inquiries about the ghosts, not easy at a police college and discovered that the former librarian who now lives in Germany had frequently heard children laughing and playing around her as she worked. A colleague of hers told me she found this delightful as there was such a happy atmosphere. I didn't probe too deeply but I hear unofficially the children play on.

The ties that bind parents and child after death may have started long before birth as Norah told me: 'As soon as I was pregnant, I knew that I was carrying a boy. I had no medical evidence for this.

'On and off throughout pregnancy, it seemed to me that I was visited by my son to be. I can only describe this by explaining that it felt as though I was not alone (when apparently I was) or if I was in company that an extra presence was with us.

'Over the nine months of my pregnancy, I began to pick up on certain qualities or characteristics to get a sense of what my son would be like and found these to be quite accurate after he was born and had begun to display more of his personality to us.

'On the day Joel was born, we went for a walk to get some contractions moving. While we were walking, I found myself overcome with a mixture of fear and sadness. It centred around the fear that at the end of this particular pregnancy there was not going to be a baby for me. At the time, it seemed totally irrational although very real and I put it down to hormonal changes.

'Joel died in November, totally unexpectedly from a cot death. Finding him dead shocked me to the core and yet looking back on his last week alive, it seems to me now that both he and I knew his life was about to end. When he died he was about six-and-a-half months old.

'Though he was taking some solids, he was still

breastfeeding. I loved feeding him and he never showed any signs that he was losing interest. Then one morning about five days before his death, he refused.

'He wasn't unhappy or ill. He would take formula milk or even my milk so long as it was from a bottle. I was absolutely distraught. It felt as though he was rejecting me, leaving me, telling me our special time together was over.

'I said to my husband, Doug, "I feel as though I'm grieving", and that's how it was over the next few days.

'After Joel died, I felt grateful to him for weaning himself like that. It seems clear to me that he was beginning to separate himself from me, preparing us both and especially me for his death.

'Having had to do some letting go of him that week definitely softened the wrench that I felt when he died. On the morning of his funeral, I drained the last of my milk and poured it down the sink.

'On the day before he died, I can see, looking back that there were definite messages for me that it was going to be his last day.

In the mornings, I usually got on with the household chores while Joel played in the same room. This normally seemed fine for both of us, but that day, it kept coming to me again and again, like a voice in my head that I should forget about the chores for that day and just enjoy being with Joel.

'There was a softness around us both that day, I felt quite mesmerised by him and dreamy and spent more time than usual with him.

'Evening came and he'd got quite grubby but I was

behind with supper and getting ready to go out so I decided to leave him as he was and clean him up in the morning. While I was cooking I suddenly remembered a saying of my mum's that you should always go out in clean underwear in case you had an accident.

'Suddenly I felt I had to clean Joel up. I lay him by the fire in the kitchen and bathed him from head to toe which he loved. As I dressed him in clean clothes I explained to him I wouldn't have wanted anyone to see him looking so dirty.

'There was no reason for me to suspect at the time that anyone would see him like that. It may seem like a small detail, but it was a source of great relief to me that when we took him to the children's hospital, the next day, he was looking clean and cared for and that he had not died dirty.

'After we'd had our supper, I gave Joel his last bottle. Often he would reach up with one hand and pull at my hair in quite a rough way, but on this night he was quite different.

'As he sucked earnestly on his bottle, he reached up with one hand and stroked the length of my face, running his fingers over my eyes, nose, mouth and hair in a very adult and loving way, very slowly and carefully, gently repeating the movement many times. I had a crick in my neck, because my head was bent for him to reach it, but I could not bring myself to move in case I interrupted this moment.

'Again there was a voice in my head reminding me to enjoy him for now.

'It seems to me that he was reminding himself of my face, touching me one last time as though he also knew he was saying goodbye. Later Doug was settling Joel down for the night when I had an overwhelming desire to have a cuddle. Part of me said this was ridiculous, that I would unsettle him just as he was going off to sleep.

'It was so strong that I stopped Doug from putting him down and picked Joel up for one last hug.

'Ever since Joel's birth, he had been my alarm. The next morning we woke late than usual and there was silence. I said to Doug, "What about Joel?" and even before Doug went into his room, I knew he was dead.

'For his coffin, we had a cross made of white roses and carnations. After the funeral we brought it home and put it by the front door. One day I came in and touched one of the roses and I thought of Joel. Suddenly something burst into life. It seemed to come into being from within me and around me at the same time and just kept expanding to fill the whole hallway I felt full of joy and ran up the stairs to the room where Joel had died.

'I couldn't see anything, yet I sensed this Presence as being warm and golden. I "knew" that it was Joel and remember being astonished because I had still thought of Joel as being a baby and realised that now he wasn't at all.

'My husband also received a visit from Joel in the week that followed his death and also experienced a very large presence, not that of a little baby. There was a very strange quality to the days that followed Joel's death.

'On one level it was a nightmare too awful to be true. Yet the engulfing darkness of those early days were pierced somehow by a light, a feeling of grace in the house and around us.

'We lost our baby, but we gained in knowledge.

Finding Joel's dead body, collecting his ashes and seeing this plastic bag of charcoal that was all that was left of our beautiful son. And yet, on another level, I knew beyond a trace of doubt that Joel's life was not at an end, but somehow a beginning.

'It is as though in dying, in making a transition from the physical to the spiritual, Joel opened up a door for me between these two realities.'

Norah wrote to me some months later to tell me that she had given birth to a daughter:

'Of course there was a lot of fear about Kailash's survival after the loss of Joel at such a young age,' she told me.

'One time when I was feeling particularly worried I had a dream in which Kailash had nearly all of her teeth and she was showing them to me. I found this dream very encouraging and took it as a sign that she is going to make it. I do believe that this dream was a communication from her to reassure me and put me at ease.

'But of course many people would say this was rubbish. To me it's obvious that there will be a bond between mother and child.

'After all before they are born they are part of us. I think that the psychic bond is like a spiritual umbilical cord that is never cut but for some it's a more open, free-flowing channel than others.'

Robbie was still a young teenager when he died from a brain tumour. His mother, Margaret, who lives in Berkshire, told me: 'The loss of a child, who one minute was dancing up and down in front of you and organising games for all the kids, then is struck down by an obscene growth in his head. How can you accept such a loss unless there is something more beyond this life?

'So much life and fun as Robbie had must go on beyond the grave. With old people, you can say that at least they lived their lives, but with a child it's not fair, he hasn't had a chance.'

He was 13 when an operation first revealed the extent of the tumour. His surgeon said there was nothing they could do and that Robbie had six months to live. Margaret took him home but he had to go back to the Royal Marsden for radium treatment.

Although she was a trained nurse, Margaret decided to take him to a psychic healer. As she said, 'at that stage, you try anything'.

On the way home, Robbie was very quiet. 'You're not going to believe this, mum,' he said. 'I was lying there. You know the pictures of Jesus with the cloak. He was standing there. I looked at his face.

'He opened his cloak and both my grandads were standing there. I was absolutely terrified and closed my eyes.

'When I opened them they were still there. It's stupid! Why should I see my grandads when they're both dead?

'She put me on my tummy and gradually I was half awake and realised someone had come and put a hand on my back between my shoulders. It was warm. I knew it wasn't Eileen [the healer]. I thought as I had seen Jesus, it might have been him, but that's silly, isn't it?'

Margaret's husband nearly went up the wall. 'It must be the drugs,' he insisted.

The drugs that Robbie had to start taking gradually

destroyed the nerves in his ears and legs. Said Margaret: 'I used to put my hands round his head. He said it felt lovely and warm. But I could feel the obscene tumour in his head and I had the feeling I couldn't heal him, though it always made him more settled.

'Even when he was very ill and he lost his hair and finger and toe nails and could not walk properly, he was out playing football until a month before he died, when he was home. He would go to head the ball and I would yell through the window: "Robbie, your head!" He would grin and field the ball with his shoulder.'

Robbie's tumour was spreading down the brain stem. Margaret used to take him to a London healer as well, determined to try anything that would help. When Robbie left the healer, he would say: 'The trees are so green, I can see colours again.'

On the Guy Fawkes night after his operation, he said to Margaret 'Why didn't you tell me that fireworks were coloured?' and she realised that for years he must have been seeing in black and white.

Margaret lost faith in the healer after she was told, while waiting for the results of Robbie's latest brain scan: 'You will be thrilled with the results of the scan. Robbie will be fine.' But when they went back to the hospital, the doctors said they were sorry, Robbie only had four months left.

But as Robbie had lasted far longer than the original medical prognosis and remained active when he should have become paralysed she feels the healing from various sources was not in vain.

What Margaret condemns is the raising of false hope.

103

'It is wrong to offer hope of a miracle.'

Robbie never knew he was dying. Margaret said he could not cope with it. On one occasion a misguided priest had gone into his room and told him that he should prepare himself for death.

The boy was absolutely terrified and ran to find his mother, throwing his arms around her and sobbing: 'I'm not dying, am I mum?' Margaret threw the priest out and managed to reassure Robbie.

On new Year's Eve, the family were playing cards at home when Robbie cried: 'Mum there's something terrible in my head.' His body had no temperature control and after three days of dreadful fits, he was admitted to hospital again. They said he could not last the night, but he continued to have fits almost continuously for 56 hours, yet survived.

At this stage he no longer recognised his mother, calling her the 'nice lady who comes to see me'. He still recognised his dad.

Unable to bear any more, Margaret went to the hospital chapel. Opening a bible at random, she saw the quotation: 'The Lord shall give thee one more day' She went back to the ward to hear Robbie saying: 'There's my mum. I'd know her footsteps anywhere. Hello mum.' It was then she realised that he had gone blind.

Fortunately his sight came back and Margaret considers it a small miracle that he knew her till the end.

His memory went at one time so Margaret left notes pinned to his pillow to tell him where she had gone. Even then she would find him wandering down the corridor, distressed and looking for her.

He began to have trouble with his left hand. Then his chemical balance went and he was ragged with dehydration. After three days, Margaret asked the nurse to sedate him as nothing more could be done.

The nurse insisted that Margaret had a rest so she wandered over to the parents' flat and started to iron her husband's shirt for the next day. A tune kept running through her head.

At first she couldn't place it then she realised it was 'The day thou gavest lord is ended'. She left the shirt and rushed to Robbie. It was the start of the rundown to his death. He remained alive from Friday night until Monday morning. On Sunday night, Margaret sat all night by his bed. There was no response, but whenever she took her hand away, he grabbed it hard. Then Robbie was gone.

Three days after his death, Margaret believes she saw Robbie in his bedroom. He was wearing what the family used to jokingly call his Rupert Bear trousers. He was getting something off the top of his tallboy where he kept all his treasures.

He had grown. The radium treatment had stopped his spine growing so his legs had grown but not his body. Now he appeared to have grown normally. He smiled at Margaret who was so shocked she burst into tears and ran away.

Lindsey, Robbie's four-year-old sister also says she saw her brother after his death. She was nearly 14 when I last spoke to her, but could still remember Robbie coming back to see her. 'Before he died, Robbie was always organising games for us,' she told me. 'He was great fun. Sometimes we use to play schools and he would be the teacher. He was always making us laugh.

'Once at the old house, after Robbie died, the girl next door used to take my best friends away to her house, so I would be left with no one to play with. I would be wandering round the house with nothing to do. If I was by myself, Robbie would usually turn up. I would talk to him and play with him. He used to make me laugh.

'When I was six or seven and we had moved to our new house, I went into my friend Nick's sitting room. Nick said, "I'll get my new train set" and disappeared upstairs. I heard someone coming downstairs a few minutes afterwards, I thought it was Nicky and I said, "Hurry up."

'When I looked round, it was Robbie sitting next to me. I told Nicky, but he made fun of me and told my mum, "Guess what Lindsey said she saw at my house".

Margaret and her husband moved into a house in a different area, which Robbie had seen, but never been in. When he had been alive, Robbie was always the first into his parents' bedroom in the morning every Christmas, birthday, Mother's Day and Father's Day to ask eagerly, 'Is it time yet?' and waking them by bouncing on the bed. After Robbie died, this did not stop, says Margaret. The first time it happened, her husband thought it was Margaret who had got up early to make a cup of tea, but she was still in bed.

Every special occasion, Margaret says she feels the pressure of the bed going down. Often things on the television would be rearranged. Robbie was always teasing his mum and would walk along in front of her, mimicking her.

Her husband hated her to wear curlers in bed and used to say, 'If I woke up and saw you like that I'd die with fright.' It was a family joke.

One night, after Robbie had died, Margaret had a special interview the next day and was anxious to look her best. So she pinned up the front of her hair and was putting on a net to hold it in place.

As she surveyed herself in the bathroom mirror, she heard Robbie's voice in her ear. 'Now who's going to frighten who then?' It was exactly Robbie's humour.

As Margaret said: 'All that life and fun couldn't be here one minute and then just gone.'

I had been talking to Margaret in the kitchen of her house. Her daughter, Lindsey, had been playing with my daughter, Miranda, who was then three years old, not far off the age that Lindsey was when Robbie died.

On the way home, Miranda said to me: 'I liked the swing in the garden.' When I telephoned Margaret some time later, I mentioned this. 'We haven't got one in this garden,' she said. 'We used to have one at the old house though.'

Chapter Seven

Don't Step On My Invisible Friend

A S MY CHILDREN have grown up, so their invisible friends have faded or changed. Jack and Miranda have replaced the squirrel family and Mr God who rode in a hot air balloon turning the sky off at night, with a complex joint mythology involving Iceman who lives in the clouds and drives his chariot across the sky and sea at sunrise and sunset.

Bill, now six, has had an assortment of invisible companions. Scarecrow, perhaps inspired by the Wizard of Oz, was half-friend and foe. He endured on and off for two years and had the inconvenient habit of taking baths when someone desperately needed the loo. Bill's current invisible companions are Skelly Bones and Wizard who live behind a blocked off panel at the top of the stairs. They are very busy characters and Bill pays nocturnal visits to their office where Skelly Bones and Wizard invent various machines with incomprehensible names. Occasionally they enjoy trips to the cinema (Bambi is Wizard's favourite film), but Wizard and Skelly Bones put on disguises and make themselves invisible so Bill doesn't have to pay for their seats.

This is neither exceptional nor anything to worry about. Separate studies by Elizabeth and John Newson, the psychologists who studied four-year-olds in Nottingham, and the Yale Guidance Nursery have shown that about a fifth of young children seem to have permanent invisible companions. This seems to depend more on the child's temperament rather than on loneliness. Among, gifted children the proportion rises steeply.

The psychologist, Lewis Terman, found that of 554 gifted children aged between five and 13, 72 per cent of girls had permanent invisible companions and 37 per cent of boys. Perhaps intelligent, creative children find they have less in common with their contemporaries and find companions they create more satisfying. And as the Newsons point out: invisible friends always score over real ones in that they are always available, always friendly and will go away without ever getting offended.

We have to be sure that the invisible friends are only figments of a childish imagination. So it would be rather alarming if one evening we parents saw Skelly Bones coming out of the wall for his nightly round. The evidence that some invisible friends might be more than just imagination is not quite as dramatic as that but it is well worth considering.

Jan, now a mother of three, still believes in the existence of her childhood invisible friend, a girl named Jellot.

Her first recollection of Jellot is when she was sitting in a huge black pram. 'Jellot was pushing the pram with my mother. My mother told me I used to point at the empty space at the end of the pram.'

Jan's mother has always been very worried by Jellot and has emphasised that Jan's friend was imaginary. The Newsons found that some mothers were disturbed by their children's invisible friends. A few feared it might be a sign of mental instability. But where a mother was prepared to accept a child's fantasies at face value and enter into his or her imaginative world, they said, she might stimulate further fantasies or develop those the child already had.

This is not necessarily a bad thing. For children to grow up confident and with a sense of worth, they need to have all their experiences treated with the importance they attach to them.

Jan next remembers Jellot when she was two or slightly older in 1950 or 1951. 'There were two air raid shelters at the bottom of the garden. I used them as a Wendy house. Jellot lived in the shelters. I used to have to walk her back there when she had come shopping. I can still visualise her clearly. She wore clothes that weren't like mine, old-fashioned and her brown dress used to come below her knee. You could see it under her coat which she always kept buttoned up even at the table. She wore a double-breasted camel coat with a collar. It was a rich material. She had brown shoes with buttons. The coat was soft to touch.'

Jan used to try to make her mum hold her hand out for Jellot when they went out and used to scream because she wouldn't. Her aunty did though and dad would lay a place at the table sometimes for Jellot. Jan says that Jellot's hand felt warm to her and could be held like anyone else's. Jellot always had one sock rolled down and had curly blonde flyaway hair. When Jan played with the other kids in the street, Jellot would come. 'When it was Jellot's turn to skip, the kids used to turn the empty rope. They tolerated her and I was under the impression they must be able to see her because I could.'

The willingness of the other children in the street to accept Jellot's existence is not in itself proof of her reality. Children are usually quite happy to share the fantasy worlds of others. But some evidence came later.

'One day I was sitting with mum in our small front room, listening to Listen With Mother on the radio. I was about four. I remember mum was knitting a pink cardigan. There was a knock at the door and I went to answer it. Mum told me off for wandering away. "I thought you were listening to your programme," she protested. She hadn't heard the knock. I turned the big handle. Jellot was standing there with a woman.

' "Oh hello, Jellot," I said. "Yes, I'll tell mum. Mum, why has Aunty Bea died? [She was the old lady who lived across the road.] Yes, she has. Aunty Bea's sister [also dead] came with Jellot to tell me so I wouldn't be worried if I found out and didn't know".'

Jan says she has no idea how she knew it was the old lady's sister. 'Mum told me not to be silly and that night she told Dad that Aunty Bea had died and I must have heard it from someone. Funnily enough, after Listen With Mother, mum went over the road and saw the old lady's next door neighbour and asked her if she'd seen the old lady. She hadn't, which was unusual.

'The neighbour came over in the afternoon to say that Aunty had died in the night.'

How could Jan have known that Aunty Bea was dead if no one else knew?

Jellot began to fade out of Jan's life when she started school. 'I didn't have time to go down to the air raid shelters any more. Then when I was seven they took down part of the shelters and she didn't come any more.'

But if Jellot had faded, 30 years later another invisible friend entered Jan's life. Her son, Ian, had a companion who appeared to come from the France of several hundred years ago. Because her mother had been so discouraging about Jellot, Jan was determined that it should be different for Ian and she came to regard the invisible Andrix (the spelling of his name is phonetic) as almost another child.

Andrix first appeared when Ian was no more than 14 or 15 months old. He used to sit on the floor playing an handing toys to someone who was not there. Jan points out that Ian was not a solitary child, since he had a brother Robert who was 14 months older and later, a younger sister. But of the three, only Ian had an invisible playmate.

When Ian was three, he tried to tell Jan what Andrix was wearing. They had a velvet pile settee and Ian used to run his fingers down the pile and say: 'That feels like Andrix's coat — that looks like Andrix's coat.' Jan says he was referring to the different colours you get when you smooth the pile. Andrix wore short trousers to the knee, very thin socks and shiny shoes. Ian told his mother Andrix was French. 'How can you understand French then?' asked Jan 'When you go to the other side everyone talks the same language,' replied Ian, who was not more than four.

Jan said a few French words to Ian to see if he understood them but he didn't. The family first went to France when Ian was five and Andrix told Ian that if he went to France now, people would not understand him.

One evening, she found Ian apparently talking to Andrix in his bedroom, saying: 'It's all right, she's downstairs. She can't hear you. No, she won't come up, honestly.' When talking to Andrix, Ian would leave the gaps as if Andrix was replying. The next morning, Jan found all Ian's toy cars with their bonnets up. Ian explained: 'Andrix doesn't know what an engine is so I have to show him. They didn't have engines in those days. There wasn't an engine on horses, but you have horse power don't you?'

Jan's husband used to make model planes and Ian had several, including a model of Concorde, on display in his bedroom. 'The next evening,' says Jan, 'I heard a noise, but didn't investigate. The next morning the nose was broken off Concorde. I was cross with Ian as he was not destructive. Ian was really upset. "Andrix did it," he insisted. "He was trying to find the engine and tried to lift the bonnet and it broke."

' "But planes don't have engines under the bonnet," I explained.

' "I know that," said Ian, "but Andrix felt there would be." '

When Robert was six, he was given a fountain pen to improve his writing. This pen apparently fascinated Andrix who told Ian he used to write with feathers, though Ian did not know what a quill pen was. One morning Jan found a squashed ink cartridge and ink all over Ian's bed and room. But, she said, there was not a drop of ink on Ian. 'Andrix was trying to find out how it worked,' Ian explained.

When Ian was three he suddenly came out with the words, uncommon for a child of his age, 'cart ruts'. Andrix had told him that he had once fallen into a cart track. Ian recounted that the roads were always muddy in Andrix's time and told about putting sacking under the cart wheels to stop them sticking in the ruts. Andrix was crossing over the road when he tripped on the ruts. 'It was very deep mummy,' Ian said. 'The mud actually came up to his waist.'

I asked Jan if Ian ever saw the Three Musketeers or similar programmes on television when he was young. She said, no, they didn't have television on much when he was that age and anyway he grew up on a diet of Thomas the Tank Engine. Certainly they had not been to France when Andrix first appeared and she cannot remember them specially talking about it.

Once Ian started school, he began to go to sleep earlier. He said that Andrix got very angry and used to say: 'You don't want to be my friend any more,' Ian would reply: 'I do, but I'm tired and have to go to school in the morning.'

Andrix disappeared for three months and then suddenly one evening Ian started playing with him. Then he disappeared for a while, came back, then came no more. Jan dates his final disappearance to the time they moved to their present house when Ian was seven.

Ian was 13 when he talked to me about Andrix in July, 1989. 'Andrix spoke French and another language so that everyone could understand him. He was always my best friend. I could see him and feel him. Whatever happened in the day, if I was told off and if I was angry with dad or in a bad mood, if I was sad and sent to bed, I could tell Andrix and he would put it all right by the morning.

'He had brown hair with a queer parting flicked over to the left side. Andrix solved all my problems. I would run to my bedroom and draw a picture of whoever I had fallen out with. Andrix told me to cross the person out and then in the morning it would be all right.'

Jan sees the invisible friends as entirely positive and says that Andrix gave the family serenity and tranquillity and had a calming presence, just as Jellot had been in her own family thirty years before.

Neither Jan nor her family are Spiritualists. But their feelings about their invisible friends parallel the spiritualist belief that invisible friends can be companions from the spirit world. Ann Bennett of Gloucester Spiritualist church told me about the spirit who was close to her son and daughter from early on. 'My daughter saw him on several occasions. When she was small, they had very high bunk beds. Once when she was small she was very feverish. I was amazed, the next morning to find her better. She told me that in the night, "A black man came to see me." He must have been very tall to reach her on the top bunk.

'She kept on about him through her childhood and was later told by a medium that a tall, coloured gentleman called Theobald was looking after her.'

A phantom friend of a different type came to Debbie's home in Nottingham home. she told me: 'I live in a mid-terrace house that is about 110 years old. When my son Adam was eight months old he would point at things in his bedroom that weren't there. As he got older, I would hear him talking to himself in the bedroom.

'When he was nearly three, I asked him who he was talking to and he said "Stephen". I said: "Why doesn't Stephen come down to the kitchen and chat to me?"

'Adam said: "He's only allowed to go in the bedroom and the bathroom."

'It was summer and I asked if Stephen wore shorts. Adam said: "Well he's got sort of short trousers, long socks and a felt cap." '

There are some strange details in this story, but so far nothing that could not be explained away by references to the usual childhood invisible friends and a good imagination. This changed when Adam was about two years old.

'One night I heard him walking round. When I went upstairs, his eyes were closed. There were toys everywhere as usual, but he was holding out his hand as if he was holding someone and stepping over the toys. Then he turned round, put his hand by his side and went back to bed.'

Who was guiding Adam round the room? A clue came from Debbie's next child, Chloe, when she was 18 months old. 'She was sitting in the bath. We used to play a game "Do you love mummy do you love daddy" and she would answer according to who was the flavour of the month.

'One day I said, "Who do you love?" and she said, "That man over there."

'I said, "What man?" She pointed to the left of me and said "That man, mummy——can't you see him?" as if I was stupid.

'One day I was in the kitchen and my husband said he'd

pop to the phone box to ring his sister. I heard him go out but a few minutes later I heard footsteps along the landing going towards the bathroom. I said to Adam, "Oh, daddy's forgotten his change."

'My son called but there was no answer. Ten minutes later my husband came back. He'd been out all the time.

'One of my husband's friends came not long afterwards with his daughter who was about two. He left her downstairs with me while he went up to the toilet. Suddenly I heard a huge shuddering sound from the bathroom.

'Ian appeared at my side white as a sheet. He said: "Debbie, there was someone behind me. He saw the reflection of a man in the picture above the toilet. After that he refused to use our bathroom even to take his daughter to change her nappy.'

Under certain conditions, a mother can actively help her child to construct an imaginary companion, with promptings and elaborations. Helen Manning, a children's psychotherapist, considered that such joint constructions might have the pay-off of providing company for the child and result in a closer relationship between mother and child.

Whether or not they can help to heal the body or offer good advice in times of trouble, the value of invisible companions would seem to be great in helping the child to cope with both social and emotional difficulties. Even the child expert Piaget who believed imagination stemmed only from what he had lived through and that the child grew out of fantasy as he became intellectually adapted to the real world, admitted the value of imaginary companions. His daughter Jacqueline, had among other friends, a strange bird-like creature which helped her in all she learned, gave her encouragement and consoled her when she was sad.

Dr David Lewis who lives in Shrewsbury wrote to me about his magic birds: 'I was born in Burma in 1948. My father was a missionary clergyman. I have no conscious memories of Burma but remember my grandmother's large house in Fordingbridge in Hampshire where we stayed for a few months after returning home pending my father's appointment to the incumbency of St Gluvias, Penryn in Cornwall.

'St Gluvias had a typical large vicarage with about two and a half acres of wildly uncontrolled garden. Perhaps an acre of this was wooded copse with mature oak, ash, lime and other full-sized trees and dense bushes, brambles and dense undergrowth. My sister was about three years younger.

'I had as my bedroom a large first floor room with a bay window looking directly towards 'the jungle'. As I lay in bed in the darkness I remember seeing the dark outlines of the trees through the uncurtained window. In the trees I saw something which I called coloured birds. They were luminous creatures about the size of birds which moved occasionally through the branches. When they moved they left a trail of light which soon faded. There were many of these birds through the field of view framed by the window and always one or two on the move.

'I remember the vivid colours and a curious depth and beauty of the creatures and the wonder and excitement I felt which I felt at the time. I never got out of bed to look more closely. I remember saying to myself, "I'll look in the morning" and promptly falling asleep.

'I never thought of these creatures as angels in spite of my devout environment. I cannot remember telling my mother then but years later I described them. My mother said I was probably dreaming of the parrots in the jungle.

'This I accepted but then I read a description of psychic globules of light playing around and on trees and plants during the hours of darkness and I now wonder if my child's mind caught a glimpse of this.'

Animals are popular invisible friends though in the case of Ellen she had a helpful farmer as well. Jean who comes from Doncaster told me: 'My seven-year-old daughter Ellen has a invisible friend she calls Farmer Fields. Recently her teacher gave the class a spelling test then realised she'd given the children the wrong test, one that was intended for the class a couple of years above. To her surprise, my daughter who is no great speller was the only child to get all the answers right. Ellen didn't tell her teacher the reason but explained to me: "It was easy. Farmer Fields whispered all the answers to me."

'Farmer Fields, according to Ellen, runs a invisible farm that doesn't have ordinary animals but gryphons and unicorns. One morning we were going to school when she stopped by a field and started to cry. "The fire is burning the field and my unicorns are sick. They are going into their realm," she told me.

'Next morning when we passed by the field, it was on fire. The farmer was burning his stubble.'

Judy, who lives in Hertfordshire, wrote: 'My son Mark is 22 and not one for delving into the realms of fantasy. A few years ago our family cat died aged 18. We were talking about her and how Mark had seldom picked her up although he'd often spoken to her and seemed very fond of her. He suddenly said, "Well she told me not to pick her up when I was little." This was from a six foot three, rugby-playing teenager. No one dared question him further.'

Angie Steele wasn't allowed to talk of her invisible friend at home but her sister was: 'My sister's invisible friend was a boy called Arby who lasted for several years until she eventually made friends with a real little boy called Harvey when she was about seven. My sister's friend was out in the open and my mum knew all about Arby and allowed him to sit at the table and go places with us. But my invisible friend had to be secret.

'Mine didn't even have a name, maybe that's why, and I don't even know if it was a boy or girl for sure. I wasn't lonely as I had a big sister and lots of friends but my invisible friend was special and always with me though I was very careful never to answer him if he spoke when anyone else was around, which sometimes happened. I wondered later if my friend had been the little girl next door who had been killed in a car accident just before we moved in. It was strange and very hurtful having to hide my friend when Arby was so welcome but mum got very annoyed if I so much as mentioned my friend and told me not to be a baby.'

Yet Angie's own mum Hilda had seen a dog who wasn't there in her own childhood as she told me: 'When I was eight or nine I went to stay with my Aunt Muriel who lived in Peterborough. In the middle of the night a big black dog leapt on my bed and I was terrified. Next morning I told Aunty Muriel and she said I was describing a labrador dog of theirs who had died three years before. That was my first psychic experience though it was so solid and real it never occurred to me it might be a ghost.'

I was told the story of one man with invisible friends, Nick, now, 35, who spent 10 of his middle years in hospital diagnosed as a paranoid schizophrenic. A glib diagnosis would be that Nick's story about his invisible friend is a sign that he did develop a dual personality. Whether his condition was caused by his childhood problems or whether he had a predisposition to mental illness is a matter for psychiatrists. But his story is quite moving. At a very early age, he was taken to Canada by his mother to find his father, a Canadian working in Winnipeg. When Nick was two, his parents married and for a time they were happy.

After Nick's first day at school which he was six, he saw a boy standing at the bottom of his bed wearing a school cap and a badge. Nick remembers the badge had a thick J with a thin S coiling round it like a snake. 'Who are you?' he asked.

'I'm your friend,' replied the little boy.

They spent hours playing together but the friend said Nick must not tell his parents because it was a secret. He kept saying 'In England we do this . . . in England we wear that . . . ' Nick asked what he was doing in Canada if he went to school in England. The boy replied, 'You brought me with you from England. When you go back, we shall go back together.'

Nick's mother died in an accident when he was about seven-and-a-half. After the funeral, Nick found his invisible friend standing in his bedroom with a suitcase. Nick's dad was working as a ranch hand and could not keep him so after six months he was sent to stay with his grandparents in England. Nick travelled alone except for his invisible friend. When the boat arrived in England, the boy got off the boat as well and Nick never saw him again.

Cathy, diagnosed as a manic depressive, was in a mental hospital for 28 years. She says that from the age of two-and-a-half she had two invisible girl friends. One had very dark hair, which had been cut short because she had nits. The other girl had long blonde hair with a blue bow which the dark-haired girl was always trying to get. Her mum used to shout at her for jigging about in the middle of the room but Cathy says she was only trying to stop them fighting over the bow.

Cathy's invisible friends disappeared when she went to school which was a relief as she had been worried about how to stop them fighting in class. Cathy's friends would say to her: 'Did you know there was dust under that vase?' or 'Did you know the cat has scratched the curtains?' She would tell her mother who would then blame Cathy saying, 'You must have done it if you knew about it'.

But the majority of children who have invisible friends grow up without problems. When Luke who lives in Reading was four-and-a-half he became obsessed with an invisible friend called Derek. Pat, Luke's gran, told me that Luke chatted almost non-stop to him about everything under the sun. Liz, his mum, became very frightened so Luke talked mainly to his gran about Derek. Pat told me: 'I asked Luke if I could talk to Derek but Luke replied, "Derek says he doesn't like nannies."

'Luke told me that Derek had been badly burned during

the war and I wondered whether Derek could be the spirit of a wartime child as Luke's house was an old one and I had often sensed strange things there. Then Derek disappeared and Luke didn't talk to him or about him any more. I understood because when I was no more than three or four years old myself, I had a very special invisible friend called Barbara Jean.

'Unlike Luke who is one of four I was very lonely as a child and Barbara Jean was my dearest friend. I can still recall Barbara Jean going up the alleyway to school with me. It was very dark and overhung with trees especially in winter and I was terrified of witches. Barbara Jean stayed with me till I was about six though I didn't dare to talk to Mum about her as she told me such things were all nonsense and got very cross with me when I mentioned my friend.'

Can a childhood invisible friend influence us in later life? When Mandy was three she had an invisible friend called Bonny who wore a white suit and worked all night on the railway. He stayed with Mandy all day. Then Mandy's Dad walked out and Mandy said that Bonny had gone as well. 'A wicked witch has taken him.'

When Mandy was 18 she met a boy called Bonny who wore a white suit. He didn't work on the railway but she fell in love with him. A coincidence? A friend returned or has she latched on to the boy because he reminded her of a time in her childhood before things went wrong?

The most exciting and perhaps elusive invisible friends are the fairy folk. Julie recalls that as a child, she had a big garden and in part of it where she played were little spirit friends who were like fairies. To Julie, they were not just pretend friends. Indeed, she says she has seen them in adult life, especially in a particular place in Devon. 'My own children have seen them too. Once when we were together we all saw them, when my son was nine and the youngest only about four.'

'What are they like?' I asked her.

'They are very fleeting, like butterflies, but not as small, about the size of squirrels.'

The most famous case of 'fairies at the bottom of the garden' is probably the Cottingley affair over which there is still controversy more than 70 years later. In 1917, cousins Frances Griffiths, aged 11, and Elsie Wright, aged 16, claimed to have played with fairies in a glen at Cottingley, in the Yorkshire dales, and produced photographs which baffled the experts including Kodak and Sir Arthur Conan Doyle, the creator of Sherlock Holmes and an ardent spiritualist. One showed a group of fairy-like figures dancing in front of a girl, the other a winged gnome-like creature near a girl's beckoning hand. Some 60 years later, the cousins admitted that four of the photographs had been faked. They had made cut-outs of fairies and placed them in the glen.

This is not the end of the story because Frances said that they did take one genuine photograph. She told Joe Cooper, the psychic researcher: 'It was a wet Saturday afternoon and we were just mooching about with our cameras and Elsie had nothing prepared. I saw these fairies building up in the grasses and just aimed the camera and took a photograph.'

Elsie insisted all the photographs were fakes. But along with Frances, she claimed that there actually were fairies.

The reason they had faked the pictures was to prove to jeering adults that the fairy folk did exist. Perhaps many of the so-called 'child frauds' do result from the demands to prove an experience. Children have been entranced by fairies for generations though they are more of a rural or at least big garden phenomena.

Pat, for example, used to see fairies, when she was about four, at the bottom of the garden belonging to the old lady who helped to bring her up. 'It was a big garden with a stream running at the bottom. They were very tiny, dressed in pink gossamer and used to play around by the stream. I told them my wildest dreams. They used to fly and hover with their tiny wings. I did not tell anyone as I knew they would have laughed.'

Recently Andrew who lives in Portsmouth told his mum he'd seen fairies at school: 'I was going to the toilet and as I went out of the classroom some fairies whizzed by me. One had a green light and one had a blue light. They were the size of the palm of my hand. The fairy beings were in the centre of the light that became paler the further away the light was from them. They went by very quickly, one in front of the other as if they were playing tag.'

Jane asked her son if the fairies said anything. 'No, mum, I told you they were whizzing by.'

To children, angels and fairies are the much same, both a source of goodness and light. Often at school the nativity play is followed by the Christmas party and a visit to Santa's grotto where the tinsel-winged creatures are not much different from those who stood round the crib. Myrtle is now in her eighties but she remembers as if yesterday her angel friends of childhood.

'When I was a child in Southern India several little angel friends used to come and play with me. In the afternoons I would be put for a rest on the verandah and they used to stand on the balustrade and come down to play if I called to them. Sometimes they stood around my mattress and told me tales of how they helped people who were in trouble, guided them over difficult mountain passes and through hazardous places and protected them from danger.

'I never told anyone my secret. It was too precious.

'When I was 13 I was sent to England to boarding school. I was so far from home and I was very miserable. But my angel friends helped me and stayed with me until I settled down. I still think about my angel friends as they were such an important part of my early life and sometimes now I feel their presence.'

In her book, *Growing Up in New Guinea,* Margaret Mead the anthropologist, writes about the Manus boys who are brought up in a culture where the spirits of the dead are a part of normal life and who at the age of four or five are given guardian spirits. The boys seem totally indifferent to their ready-made invisible friends and none of them invent any imaginary companions.

She also points out the total lack of a fantasy life among the children and likens their play to that of small animals. This is, she suggests, because no child is ever without a companion. It could also be due to the fact that the spirits revered by the parents seem very dull and restrictive, interested only in property and adult issues. But for children in the Western world, invisible friends and fairies provide companionship, comfort and even protection.

Chapter Eight

Good Fairies and Guardian Angels

G OOD FAIRIES, ANGELS and fairy godmothers are regarded by some psychologists as a children's way of coping with the fearsome elements in their lives, many of which are not real dangers, but come from their own fantasies and their sense of helplessness against powerful adults. But those who have had a helping hand from Heaven may need more than psychological arguments to convince them that divine intervention is all in the mind.

Angels can help children to feel safe and protected. My son Jack saw an angel when he was six. He told me about its visit as we were walking down to the local beach. 'I saw an angel outside my bedroom window last night, mummy. I had a bad dream and when I woke up there she was.'

'What was she like?' I asked.

'You know,' Jack said, 'like an angel, wings and a

white dress. Do you think it could be a clockwork angel?'

Jack was just leaving the magical stage and trying to explain things to himself. I said I didn't think so but asked him if he thought it was perhaps a fairy.

'Mum,' he said as though talking to a two-year-old, 'angels are angels and fairies and fairies. Can we have some crisps?'

Annette saw an angel but was very hurt when her parents didn't share her excitement: 'When I was 10, I went to stay in Glasgow with my parents. I was in bed recovering from a bout of 'flu. It was about two in the afternoon when I looked up at the wall facing my bed and I saw an angel. She was a lovely woman in a long flowing gown with long flaxen hair. She appeared to come from the outside wall and floated across the room and disappeared out of the other wall.

'I jumped out of bed to tell my mother and she said I must have been dreaming but I know I was wide awake. I remember feeling very excited when I saw the angel and wanting my parents to know. My father was cleaning his shoes ready to go to work when I rushed in with the news. The experience made me feel very special for a long time and I told my best friend I was "the chosen one". My grandma had just died and we had been very close.'

Rosemary James is a teacher and a mother in her thirties. She told me about the angel she had seen as a child. Again her mother tried to explain away her experience: 'When I was about six we were living in a rented house in Northern Ireland. It was a strange old house. I was ill in bed. The curtains were drawn but the room looked out on to the back garden. I suddenly saw a beautiful golden angel with wings. It was the size of an adult. I wasn't frightened but just lay in bed looking at the wonderful angel. I felt it was the right time to see an angel as there had been a lot of illness in our family.

'I told my mother but she completely disregarded me. It was so disappointing and she insisted that it must have been just a light shining on the side of the house. But it wasn't as there was no light for miles and I knew my angel was true.'

Mary who lives in Mid-Wales isn't sure whether her angel was dream or vision but it remains even in her adult life a very special experience: 'When I was 12 or 13 I had a dream in the middle of the night that there was a bright light shining outside my bedroom window. I got out of bed and felt my way downstairs to the room below mine to get a closer view. The curtains were not drawn because the room was rarely used. It looked out on to the garden and to the wall and the window of the convent next door. Framed as it were by the window were three angels formed of golden light rays. I do not know how long the vision lasted nor do I remember going back upstairs to bed. In the morning I felt as if it had not been a dream at all. I wasn't sleep-walking and am sure I left my bed that night.'

My favourite angel is five year old Julie's. I met her mum in a local supermarket and I got chatting about a broadcast I was going to do about angels for Christmas on radio in Ireland. When I said that lots of people didn't believe in angels, she replied: 'Well I do. Julie saw one just before last Christmas.

'My mum had died suddenly at the beginning of December and though we were making the best of Christmas for the kids our hearts weren't in it and even the children weren't excited. Then one morning Julie came thundering downstairs and told me, "It's all right, mum. I've just seen a beautiful angel, all silver with huge wings. She told me that Nanny is in heaven and is perfectly happy and says we're to have a good Christmas or else."

'So we did have a good Christmas after all and I felt my mum around the whole time which was very comforting.'

Pauline believed that a voice intervened twice on her behalf when she was a child. The first time was in 1930 when she was 10 and the fourth child of a family of eight.

She wrote: 'Dad was out of work and mother was always struggling to make ends meet. The constant worry made mother sharp-tongued and quick with a cuff round the ear if we didn't jump to do what she said. Each evening after school, it was always my job to look after my baby brother. Mother gave me instructions to take him in his pram and push him round the streets so he got some fresh air, but for once I disobeyed her.

'As soon as she disappeared into the house, I pushed baby down the yard, turned a corner where we would not be seen, I left baby safely outside and entered the old wash house. I was determined to do something an older brother had told me about the day before. I had to stand on a wobbly bucket to reach the communal cold tap that served our family and three others.

'I turned it on and put my finger inside making the water squirt all over the place. I was so engrossed in this wonderful game that I was lost to the world.

'But suddenly a loud clear voice in my ear said, "Your

mother is coming down the yard into the wash house. Get out quick."

'I was so startled that I fell off the bucket. I picked myself up and ran to where I had left the baby and we quickly hid behind the privy wall. Luckily the baby was quiet. My mother came to fill the old iron kettle in the wash house. So the voice saved me from a good hiding.'

Pauline's second voice came to help out when she was about 13. 'Dad was still out of work and things were desperate at home. He had a pair of worn-out boots, his only ones. He mended all the family's shoes expertly on an iron foot, but just could not afford to buy a sixpenny piece of leather from the cobbler's.

'I was on an urgent errand to the Co-op for three pennyworth of bacon and was thinking about Dad as I hurried along. I was walking on some broken pavement. Weeds and dock-leaves grew through the cracks. As I did, a clear loud voice said in my ear, "Look down among the dock leaves and you will find sixpence."

'I knelt down and felt inside and out the green clumps, but it was not there. Then I saw a clump growing almost out of the wall. I felt carefully around each leaf till at last I made contact with a silver sixpence. I fled with it to the Co-op and came home with a large bag of bacon pieces and a hock.

'That put a smile on mother's face. With plenty of potatoes and root vegetables, we were assured of dinner for the next two days.

'Mum and Dad accepted the story that I found the sixpence. I was brought up to be honest, but I couldn't tell them about the voice. Dad got the leather to repair his boots and soon after got a job as a drayman to the corn merchant at the mill nearby.'

Sceptics will say there was likely to be money on a well-worn path. But she did find the money exactly where she was told and it made her family very happy. I know which explanation I prefer.

After all, fairy tales don't have to be about princesses going to cottages in the woods. They can equally apply to a worried little girl on her way to the Co-op for bacon scraps.

Cicely's great-grandfather was not quite so fortunate. In the early 1860s when he was a boy, he lost his father, so had to leave school to find a job. He was apprenticed to a carpenter in the Worcester area. One day he was working on the wainscot in an empty house when he saw the figure of a man walk through the wall. He told the boss what he had seen and the carpenter took up the skirting board at that point and found a great deal of money there. Apparently the old gentleman's money had never been found when he died.

What happened to the money Cicely does not know except that her great-grandfather did not make his fortune as a result.

Sometimes guardian angels can be lifesavers. Cathy tells how she and her husband were missionaries in India for more than 20 years and lived in a very large bungalow in Punjab with very high ceilings. 'One night I put our younger son to sleep in the corner of the bedroom. He was about two years old. I went back a short time later to see if he was asleep. He was but had crawled down to the end of the bed and was lying where his feet normally would have been. I moved him back with his head on the pillow and went out again. A little later I went in and found him with his head at the foot of the bed again and moved him back again. A few minutes later there was a tremendous crash. A cornice of the ceiling had fallen on his pillow. The child was, however, unhurt, as once again he had crawled down the bed.'

Did some sixth sense warn Cathy's child that his normal sleep position was hazardous or were his repeated movements to the foot of the bed and the crashing ceiling merely separate events that coincided by sheer chance? Or did some friendly spirit or guardian angel protect him?

A relationship with an adult that was supportive in life can as far as the child is concerned sometimes carry on. Perhaps this can be dismissed as the child's imperfect understanding of the real world or perhaps in his ghost friends, he is merely externalising an inner truth, that the dead can and do still influence us long after they are gone.

Sheila's mother recalls: 'When my daughter was four of five, she was great friends with our neighbour, Mrs Tompkins. Mrs Tompkins was deaf, but she and Sheila had great conversations over the garden fence. Mrs Tompkins, a Welshwoman, listened carefully to every clear, high-pitched word of Sheila's and Sheila listened to Aunty Tompkins.

'One day I had to tell Sheila that Aunty Tompkins had died, Sheila didn't cry, but looked a little dismayed. "I wish you hadn't told me mummy. Then I wouldn't have known."

' "But you would have to know sometime," I replied and she said, "No because I still see her".

' "Do you mean with your eyes or your mind?" I asked.

' "With my eyes of course,' said Sheila. 'She's there in the garden."

'So I said, "That's all right, then, give her my love," and we left it at that. Then one night, Sheila woke up crying. "Tell Aunty Tompkins I love her, but not to stand too close to my bed. She frightens me."

'I said, "I'm sure she didn't mean to. Let's tell her." So we said aloud, "Please Aunty Tompkins, we're pleased to see you, but don't wake Sheila so suddenly. You gave her a fright."

'After that we had no more problems. Aunty Tompkins stayed in the garden except twice in Sheila's room when the child wasn't frightened at all. Then one night or early morning, Sheila called me sobbing, "Aunty Tompkins came to see me. She said she's going now. She said goodbye. I'll never see her again." I didn't know what to say except, "I'm sure you will."

'Sheila said, "No. She said, 'Well goodbye dearie. I'm, going on now, You won't see me any more, God bless'." I told Sheila we should be pleased for Aunty Tompkins.'

What is quite rare is the positive attitude Sheila's mother took, accepting the value of her daughter's experience and not feeling threatened by it or any need to disprove it. As it was. Sheila was able to work through the experience and let go at the appropriate moment.

Edna carried on a similar friendship. 'When I was little my parents kept a lock-up shop a mile from where we lived with my grandma. One afternoon, I decided to go along and join my mother. When my mother saw me, amazed and shocked no doubt that a toddler had come so far alone,

she asked: "Weren't you afraid to come all that way
alone?"

' "Oh, no," I replied, "I had Mr Taig [a friend of my
parents who had recently died] and all my dead people
with me." '

Perhaps her remarks were a bit of inspiration to get
round the parental injunction 'You must never walk up the
road on your own'. After all, Edna may well have reasoned, mum could hardly check with the people concerned. Or in a world where children are told stories about
talking rabbits who wear clothes and are warned not to go
out or the bogeyman will get them, it is not surprising the
odd dead person pops up. Or perhaps, Mr Taig did make
sure the little girl came to no harm.

A similar tale was recounted by Ruby Barnes who lives
in California. She told me that when she was seven years
old and living in Nevada her stepmother had to go into
hospital for a sudden operation. Her Aunt Carrie whose
house she had only visited once when she was very young
was picking her up from the school playground to take her
home on the other side of the city.

'My aunt was late so I decided to find my own way but
in a few minutes I was completely lost and terrified in an
unfamiliar part. I prayed for help and a voice told me to
follow it and I would be shown the way. I wasn't worried
any more and followed the directions I was being given.
I arrived at my aunt's home to find a total panic. My aunt
was there very upset and search parties were out looking
for me. No one could believe I could possibly have found
my way as I didn't even know the address.'

Carole who lives in Reading told me: 'As a small child,

there were three holes in my bedroom curtain. Through the holes I could see a big blue eye. I knew from them there was someone out there looking after me. The eye wasn't always there. Sometimes I could just see the moon.

'My grandparents lived next door. I remember when I was six or seven I was sent next door with a message. It was teatime and winter so though it was only about five o'clock it was pitch black. It seemed such a long way from their gate and through the dark entry to their back door.

'I stood at the back gate frozen with fear and can remember saying, "I can't get there".

'Suddenly I was lifted off the ground by someone I couldn't see, carried all the way to the back door and put down gently. I didn't tell anyone because I felt it was a very special thing. Afterwards I was much less scared because I knew for sure I was being looked after.

'When I was about eight, I fell out of a tree. I was with my cousins Gill and Peter in the garden of a pub by the River Thames. I had climbed the tree and was quite high up when I lost my grip and I fell backwards horizontally. As I fell, I cried to my guardian angel, "Please come and help me".

'Afterwards my cousins said it was as if I fell in slow motion and landed not with a bang but as though there were cushions under me. I got up with hardly a scratch or bruise where I should have been really badly hurt. Again I knew I was being taken care of. But I made my cousins promise not to tell any of the adults who were fortunately out of sight as we'd have got into dreadful trouble for climbing the trees.'

Occasionally, however, it can be the children who

become the helpful spirits, looking after mum. The anthropologist, Margaret Mead, in *Growing up in New Guinea,* her study of the Manus tribe, says that in this culture, it is the father who is the popular indulgent figure in the family and the mother is largely disregarded by her children and indeed usually by her husband and his family as well.

That situation persisted until the death of a male child (at the time of the study in 1928 the infant mortality rate was still very high) when the mother assumed the power of medium (in many cultures pregnant women and young boys are traditionally associated with clairvoyant powers).

Margaret Mead recorded that little boys who in life stuck out their tongues at their mothers, spat, sulked or struck out at any attempts to discipline them became mother's little helpers in death. Their spirits communicated with a whistling noise (made through their mothers' lips) and these sounds can be interpreted by the mother in ways that give her a bit of clout in the family after all.

The helping hands from Heaven can work in mysterious ways, sometimes leading a child into trouble although the situation may work out for the best. June told me the story of her father, Oscar, who was born in India in 1877, the eldest child of an army chaplain. The family did not have much money and his wealthy Uncle Howard in England offered to educate Oscar on condition he could adopt the child who would take his name. Oscar's father's reaction was 'aren't we lucky' although his mother was in tears.

But his father pointed out that they would not see Oscar

for many years anyway as he would have to be sent to England for his education. Oscar and his mother, and the three younger children, travelled to England. Then, on the appointed day, dressed in his Eton suit for the first time, Oscar and took the train with his mother to Hastings where they were to meet Uncle Howard for lunch at the hotel where he lived.

Throughout the meal, the boy kept asking: 'Who are the men in the garden? Why are they wearing funny clothes?' Annoyed, Uncle Howard, sent for the gardener who said there was no one in the garden. Both the gardener and the waiter gave Oscar a funny look.

Furious, Uncle Howard said that he was not taking on a boy who told lies. As they were leaving the hotel, the waiter came up to Oscar's mother and said: 'Don't worry. He's got the sight. My father worked here before me and there were prisoners of the Napoleonic wars tied against the wall. The clothes would have been like the boy described.'

The unexpected sight of the ghosts, although they may have made Oscar appear a liar in his uncle's eyes, saved him from a potentially disastrous relationship with a man obviously unsympathetic to children. Instead, Oscar's mother and the four children stayed in Oxford where he went to school and the family lived on the 'sniff of an oil-rag' as there were two households to maintain but were very happy.

When his mother had to return to India with the younger children, Oscar, became a boarder at Marlborough School to which he had won a scholarship. During his holidays he stayed at the house of another uncle, a priest in Yorkshire.

He was very miserable in his uncle's household and always cold.

The day started with family prayers, and Oscar should have been going down for them one morning when he saw the figure of a woman in a long dress going into his aunt's room. 'There's plenty of time still if aunt has not gone down,' he said to himself and, being a dreamy boy, he dawdled around upstairs.

When he finally got downstairs, the whole household was gathered for prayer. 'I'm so sorry,' he said, 'but I just saw aunt go into her room.' There was a hush. One of his cousin's kicked him and pulled him into his place. That afternoon, he was told off by his uncle for lying.

But one of his cousins later told him that it was well known that a figure haunted the house. Oscar saw her three times during the rest of his stay there. Again, a psychic incident made Oscar realise that the relationship with this uncle was not going to work either. He began spending more of his holiday time at the house of a friend's family who were more responsive to a dreamy small boy and enabled him to follow a more creative path in life.

But the most common guardian angels are, not surprisingly, grandparents who continue to keep a benign eye on their grandchildren. The Reverend Tom Willis, a Church of England priest in Yorkshire with a great deal of experience of the paranormal, confirmed my view. 'Grans drop back to see the latest addition. If you were dead and were a granny, wouldn't you want to come back to see the new baby?

'My wife, who's a psychologist, says in her neat Irish way, "I think the dead are closer to us than we are to them.

After all they've been in both dimensions". She doesn't know if she read it somewhere, or if it's her own idea, but I think it sums ghosts up pretty well.

'Granny will often keep an eye on the children. They often report an old man or woman popping their head round the bedroom door at night to check. It is just the grandparent lending a hand.

'There is nothing wrong in that. If granny were always following you around, it would be worrying, but if she is seen looking over the cot of the newborn, that is fine. Where a woman has lost her mother before her own child is born, it may even be wish-fulfilment.

'One mum was breastfeeding the new baby in the bedroom and the five-year-old was playing with his toy car. The little boy looked up.

' "Grandad," he cried with delight. Mum looked up and saw her dad who had recently died. Grandad went downstairs and the little boy chased after him. Then he came back puzzled. "Where's grandad gone?" he asked.

'In the church we talk about the Communion of Saints, the fellowship of man with the good dead. This is the good side of the coin, the guides and protectors that are with you and will help you, if you don't dabble.'

A rational explanation for the grandparents' reappearance was suggested by Eileen Orford, a child psychotherapist at the Tavistock Clinic in London: 'A gran who has died may be held in memory as someone who is very kind. So when a child is ill or unhappy, it is natural for him to revive the memory of a loving person to care for him. I am happier about a child seeing gran than for him to start seeing angels.'

Could a child retain a memory of someone they never knew? Lindsay's mother found that she was sometimes pushed to give a demanding toddler enough attention. But it didn't matter because Lindsay had 'my other mummy'.

'I used to sit in my high chair and my other mummy used to come through the wall and sit by me,' Lindsay told me some years ago. 'She would come through the wall in my bedroom and talk to me about all sorts of things and make me laugh. She looked very much like my mum, only she wasn't.'

The identity of the other mummy remained a mystery until at a family party, Lindsay caught sight of a pile of old family photos and pounced on one with delight. 'There she is — my other mummy.' It was her great-granny in Edwardian wedding dress and almost the image of Lindsay's mother.

Lindsay's other mother always made her laugh. 'I sometimes thought she was nicer than my real mum.' No doubt the other mummy never made unreasonable requests about cleaning teeth or not making a mess. She was never too tired or too busy or had a headache. She arrived when Lindsay was bathed and in bed and had passed the miserable post-teatime rattiness from which most toddlers suffer. No wonder she was such a cheery soul.

By adulthood, this idealised person is on the whole relegated to fantasy, though there are people who go from spouse to spouse and family to family in search of perfection. They obviously didn't handle it all as well as Lindsay and her mum.

Elizabeth says her grandmother who died 21 months before she was born, used to pop in whenever she was sick as a child. 'I used to see the figure of an elderly lady, dressed in black and always wearing a little hat approach my bed, sit looking at me for a few seconds and then seem to melt away in the shadows by the door. It didn't seem to worry me. I accepted it though it certainly seemed to startle my mother and she used to say it was only my imagination or the results of a high temperature. But I knew the bedside visitor was my granny whom I had never met. The last time I saw her was when I was 14 and was very ill with bronchitis.'

It is hard to dispute when gran is fixed in her stained glass window forever smiling, apple-cheeked and white-haired. Janet Boucher, a child psychiatrist says: 'Children know that granny existed even if they didn't know her. If she has died, then mum will usually speak of her in a nice way, 'Your gran would have said this or done that. It is less likely to happen if the child has a secure relationship with mum.'

Sometimes a ghostly grandparent can be frightening if the child does not know them or does not understand the purpose of the visit. Carolyn told me: 'My neighbour Jean's dad died while she was pregnant. She was only 19 when her daughter was born and she was very distressed about him not seeing the baby. When the baby, Ann, was only a few months old, Jean would hear her giggling in her cot and when she went in, the baby would be wriggling as if she was being tickled. She would also seem to be looking at someone and smiling. Jean was convinced it was grandad.

'When Ann was three, she insisted she could see an old man standing across the road staring at the house. Her mum said there was no one there, but the little girl was very distressed. Then, Ann said the old man was on their side of the road. Again Jean told her there was no one there, but Ann was still frightened.'

The next day, fearing that there might be a strange man lurking in the area, Jean asked her neighbours if they had seen anyone out of the ordinary. The little boy next door had been telling his mum that he had seen a man in his house and would not go to bed. But the mother had seen no one.

A few days later the same boy, in tears, told his mother that the man was at the front of the house. Ann told her mother the same but if there was a man there, then only the children could see him.

'Ann said the old man had come into her garden. But then she stopped being frightened and her mum saw Ann running round the garden laughing as if she was being chased. Then, apparently the old man who only the children could see disappeared. Jean wondered if it could be her dad and if Ann had been afraid of him until he actually came to play with her in the garden.'

Rosemary was also frightened by the unexpected appearance of a grandparent: 'When I was very young, one of my aunties was taken very ill. I didn't know at the time, because we lived some distance apart and my father had quarrelled with my aunt. I awoke in the night at about two o'clock. At the side of my bed was a little old lady. She didn't say anything, just stood there. On the side of her head was a white mob cap. The only person I knew with a white mob cap was my granny, dad's mother and she had been dead for several years.

'I was so frightened that I switched on the light and slept with it on all night. I didn't tell anyone because I didn't think they would believe me. Two years later my aunty and father patched up their differences and she told us about the time she was very ill in hospital. One night, so one of the nurses told her, though my aunt was too ill to notice, a little old lady with a mob cap was sitting by her bed. The nurse later asked my aunt who the old lady could have been and my aunt said it was her mother.'

As far as Rosemary could tell this incident happened at about the same time as gran had appeared in her bedroom. Could it have been that granny knowing that her daughter was in trouble, but that she and her brother were estranged had gone to her granddaughter to try to tell her that her aunt needed help? Perhaps the old lady had hoped that Rosemary would tell her dad about her dream and that this might prompt him to contact his sister.

Laurence's grandad was a very special person in his life and it seemed when he died, he came to reassure the lad. 'I was told my father was a Canadian airman who had been killed in the war. I was brought up with my grandparents. My grandad had a stroke and could not walk unaided. He used to go to the local bowling green in his wheelchair. When I was five, my mother remarried, but we remained with my grandparents till I was nine. My parents and I moved, which I did reluctantly as I had to leave the people I had grown up with.

'When we had settled in the new house, I had a dream I was sitting at the top of the stairs with my grandad looking down the stairs. A shape which I now take to be a monk's habit with a hood moved upstairs towards us. I said to my grandfather, "It's coming," but he said, "Don't worry. It's not coming for you."

'Next day, my stepfather broke the news that my grandad had died.'

Claire believes her grandad first came back to her while she was a child and has continued to figure in her adult life. 'When I was nine, my great-grandfather died whom I loved very much. The night he died, he came to see me two hours after his death. At the time I did not know he was dead and did not understand what he was saying to me, though now I do. Every time someone dies, he comes to tell me they are all right.

'When my daughter was very ill and we all thought she was going to die, he came to tell me not to worry. She would get better and she did recover. I don't know how I would cope if he didn't come again.'

Grannies are often accused of spoiling grandchildren and leading them astray and according to Pamela, this too can continue in the afterlife.

''When I was 12 my gran died,' she said. 'The Grand National was her favourite horse race. She always had a little bet on it. The milkman used to put it on for her. The year after she died, she came to me in a dream and gave me the name of the horse who would win. I didn't say anything to anyone, but the horse won.'

Chapter Nine

The Phantom Father

MY DAD MOVED into my old room after he died and sleeps in the cupboard and looks after me,' said Emma. When we talked in the summer of 1989 Emma, the youngest of four children, was ten-and-a-half, slightly shy, and mature for her age in many ways, a perfectly ordinary child but for her belief that the ghost of her father, who committed suicide, is still there.

'I keep on feeling he is in my old room and sometimes hear him,' she said. 'There was already something there. My friend who lived here before us, said her grandad was here. Now I have my guardian angels — the ghost and my dad. I can also feel my old dog Gus. Five months back, I told the dog "Come back after you're dead so I can hug you". And he has come back.' He was her father's dog and did not long survive his master.

Neither the bustle of psychic investigators with their

paraphernalia nor the probing of a psychiatrist seemed appropriate in this welcoming home where neighbours were constantly dropping by for coffee and a chat. Whatever the truth, Emma had managed to come to terms with a situation that would floor many adults.

'Emma has been quite confused since her dad's death,' her mother Anna told me. 'She thinks he is still around and can feel his presence. Emma was at school when his body was discovered. I brought her home, but she wanted to go straight back to school. Emma's father was very cold and undemonstrative with Emma.

'There was no relationship between them. The atmosphere was cold and repressive when Emma was young. I even tried holding back my affection from the younger children in the hope he would take the initiative, but he went the other way. Emma would not even let him put her to bed, so great was the dislike between them.'

Eventually Anna told her husband that she could stand no more of his silences and coldness and wanted a divorce. He just sat around the house and refused to speak.

The day before he died the family had been planning to go on a Save-the-Whale walk organised by Greenpeace. Anna told her husband that she did not want him to come with them. He was not around when they set off but that did not surprise her as he often used to go off for long periods without telling her.

The next morning she found his body in the garage.

Emma told me: ' "I bet Dad's run off or something," I said when we got home and he wasn't there. Mum said, "Don't be silly. He's just gone for a long walk." But, next morning, he was in the garage dead.

147

"You see," I told mum, "I was right."

The ghost seems to have changed his nature from a cold, unfeeling person to a guardian angel, giving Emma the affection that he never gave in life.

Anna admits to feeling his presence once in the house but this was after an uncanny incident at the Avebury Rings, a stone circle dating back to the Bronze Age, and older than Stonehenge, just outside Marlborough, in Wiltshire.

The giant earthworks and the remains of what is believed to have been a giant sun temple encircle a cluster of buildings that form the heart of the village. It is said to stand on a ley line, one of the straight lines which appear to connect ancient monuments and which many experts of the occult believe to be a source of great spiritual energy and power, (a sort of ancient psychic national grid).

Battered by the years and by locals who tore down the stones for building materials or through fear of pagan powers they were said to possess, the remains of the Avebury Rings are less immediately impressive than Stonehenge. But in peaceful conditions they can be awe-inspiring.

However, when Anna and Emma visited them on Easter Monday, 1989, the area was packed with tourists. Mother and daughter had been on an activities weekend at a local farm. The visit was to have strange consequences.

'Avebury was very busy so I did not think I would feel anything,' said Anna. 'In the first circle, I felt quite light and good. I did not lean against any of the stones. Then we went over the road to the other circle. Immediately I was inside I felt an awful anxiety. I stood against one of the stones and felt a physical experience in my legs. It was an awful physical and emotional experience. I learned later that was the male circle and the other one was the female.

'When I stepped into the second circle, it was just like being with him again — my husband. Emma was close to me in the stones. I wanted to get away so I stepped outside, leaving Emma inside.'

Said Emma: 'In the first circle, I felt OK. I didn't touch any of the stones. I felt at home like you do anywhere. We crossed the road to the second circle. I stood against three big stones. They were about eight feet high.

'The first I stood against felt as though death was coming. I moved away quite quickly. I stepped across to the next. I felt like a swan flying.

'The third one felt nice, but not too nice for words. Mum went out and I felt dizzy because I went in the horrible one again. Something not exactly dragged me, but called my name and drew me gently and I went over. I felt really sick and dizzy.

'I ran out. "Come on," I said, "I want to go. That one's nice." The second one felt as if it was pushing against me.'

Then Emma ran from the circle, shouting, 'I really like those stones, they are nice.' But her furious tone contradicted her words. Anna said: 'You don't sound as if you like them.' And Emma became very upset. She was crying, confused and wanted to run away. Anna says it was almost as if Emma linked into the family feeling, for her anger was just like the repressed anger of her dead father.

'I'll never go there again,' she cried and 'It was nice, it was good. I felt safe there.'

'Emma's hidden anger was like being round him again,' said Anna. Emma found it very painful to talk about the incident afterwards. But the incident did seem to have some cathartic effect.

Immediately afterwards, Anna says she felt her husband in the house. It was warm, loving, comforting and encompassing, something that she had never experienced in that house before and quite uncharacteristic of him. She remembered very strongly that the last few days before his death were particularly fraught.

For Emma and for Anna, the stones seemed a focus for their confused feelings about Emma's dead father. Helen Manning, the psychotherapist, commented: 'In many cases, imaginary or ghost characters are a way of the child keeping alive the memory of the person who is absent for whatever reason. It may be painful for the family to acknowledge the person, but the person is important for the child.'

I told Emma that when my own mother died, in painful circumstances after a long and agonising illness, in contrast to her attitude I had coped with the pain and the loss by pretending to myself that she had never existed at all. If anybody mentioned her to me I changed the subject. I did this for about two years and then found that I did not need to do it any more.

So one day, I told her, you might find that you do not need your dad in your bedroom any more and when that time comes you will know. She thought that seemed quite sensible.

To the child a father can be a figure of love, or as in Emma's case, cold and an unloving. Or he can be a demon figure. J.M. Barrie, summed this up in his masterpiece, Peter Pan with Captain Hook, 'father but for the grace of god'. The dreadful Hook and Mr Darling, the head of the family, are often played by the same actor.

In another case that I came across, a young boy, Edmund, was going through a traumatic period with his father when he began to be haunted by a creature he called 'lion with glasses'.

Edmund is now 15 and the lion's reign of terror covered 18 months, from when he was about two-and-a-half until he was four. 'I remember the lion with glasses very well. He was in my bedroom in the big white house [he and his mother had moved to a new home after a reconciliation with her husband following a period of separation]. I used to be sent to my bedroom while my first Daddy was having his lunch.

'I saw the face on top of the curtains, hanging out looking over me, the lion with glasses. He was yellowy brown, he stared at me. I was very scared of him.

'He looked horribly at me as if he was going to kill me and jump out at me. I used to hide behind my wardrobe until someone came upstairs. He changed shape when people came so he wouldn't look so fierce. I knew he was real when I was small.

'I think now it was just the shape of the curtains. When the wind blew he looked bigger. He was only in that house, in that bedroom. I used to dream about him. He was really awful, horrible, in my dream. He used to peer in at my curtains. I used to try to get out of bed, but a force held me. He said, "You're going to die. I hate you for living in this house." I couldn't move. Now when I remember that, I think now perhaps he was real. The force was holding me. The lion was talking. "Nobody enters my dream". He had a horrible voice. He looked over me with his great glasses. He was just a head. Every night I had dreams about him.

'When we moved away it was completely different. It was after Christmas that he came. After we went out in the road and I got a sweet from Father Christmas on his sleigh. Then the lion said, "I hate you for living here, It's my house".

'It was not the same room in my dreams. The windows were open and the door was locked. The lion was velvety. I liked the skin of the lion with big round glasses the same colour as my dad's. He was a very realistic lion. Sometimes when the wind was blowing, his face was twisted up. Last time, I saw him he said, "I'm going". He was not there the last couple of nights before we moved.'

Edmund's mother said: 'I can remember the lion almost as well as Edmund. I had thought he came as soon as we moved to the south-west of England and a white house with big rooms, high ceilings and ornate curtain rails. It was not a happy house. It was meant to be a new start after a separation.

'I was pregnant with my second child but my ex-husband found the noise and mess of a toddler difficult to cope with. I was trying to be good wife and mother and found the two conflicted. Edmund was shut in his room while my ex-husband ate lunch. He found family meals traumatic so it seemed less stressful to feed Edmund first.

'The lion was a real problem in our lives. It was not until I left my husband and Edmund, the baby and I moved away to an old cottage in a market town about 20 miles away, that the lion went. Edmund said the lion told him he was going off. I thought we were the ones to leave the lion. Perhaps we were both right.'

Helen Manning, comments: 'It must have been a fearful time for Edmund. Change was in the air with the arrival of the baby, the parental relationship was rather uncertain. How does a child make sense of moving house, parental disharmony, new baby etc. In some way maybe this lion was the expression of the threat the child was experiencing.'

Whether or not the lion was a psychic or psychological manifestation, at the time it was terrifyingly real for Edmund. Night terrors are a well-known childhood phenomena. Melanie Klein, the psychologist, wrote that at night, when invisible foes seem at their most potent, the child can feel hemmed in by all sorts of malevolent powers, 'sorcerers, witches, devils, phantastic figures and animals' as his or her own bad thoughts come back to haunt him.

The most important aspect of night terrors would seem to be that, however improbable they might seem to adults, they should be treated seriously. A child should be able to confide in his or her parents without fear of being mocked or disbelieved.

Sometimes the child must feel like the character in a horror movie who is being stalked by a nameless dread — a vampire or some such monster — and whom everyone refuses to believe until it is too late.

Judy who lives in Hertfordshire wrote to me after she found the earlier edition of this book in her local library. She dismissed her daughter's night-time fears as fantasy.

But then she had a strange experience of her own: 'Like many of the mothers you write about, when my daughter (now 24 years old) was about two or three she had very bad dreams and I had a job getting her to stay in bed on her own.

'When my younger son reached the same age they shared a room and several times my daughter told me she'd woken in the night and seen an old lady bending over Mark's bed. I suppose I was afraid myself and told her she was dreaming. I asked her recently about this and she says she definitely wasn't dreaming.

'It's only recently I've wondered whether the lady was connected with a strange experience I had with my daughter, Sam, when she was a few months old. She was asleep in her pram in the garden and I looked out of the window and saw a woman peering over Sam. We have a back gate at the end of the garden leading to a lane as well as the conventional front entrance. I asked the woman what she wanted.

'A quarter of a century later I remember exactly what she said. "They said there was a way through here but not for me there isn't."

'I assumed at the time she'd come from the lane and wandered up our garden though there is a gate. I picked Sam up and told the woman it was a private garden and she could go back through the gate and on to the main road. I put Sam back in the pram and when I looked up the woman had disappeared. I thought no more of her going — I was very concerned at the time that a stranger could have theoretically taken my child.

'It's only later that I realised I was not conscious of her

going and heard no footsteps.'

The psychic world is like a jigsaw puzzle and Judy will never know whether the old lady was, as she wonders 'a dotty old lady who lost her way' or Sam's lady who perhaps was still trying to find her way centuries on.

Often a child will not share his fears even with his brothers and sisters. Mark who lives in Newport in Wales told me on a radio phone-in programme: 'When I was no more than six I used to hear the sound of a man breathing in my bedroom. I mentioned it to my mum and dad and they said it was just my sisters snoring next door but it wasn't.

'The sound was different and always came from behind a very old dressing table and stopped when the family got rid of the dressing table. I mentioned it 20 years later to my sister and she said that she had heard the sound when she had that bedroom and my other sister had heard it too when she had the room.

'The strange thing was none of us had mentioned it to the others as children. I used to get my torch out from under my pillow and go and investigate. Now I don't know how I had the nerve.'

Ivy felt that she had to face her fears alone. 'I think I would have been seven years old when I lived in sheer terror in our farmhouse. It was quite a lonely house, way up in the hills, directly on the Pennine Chain. I never told my parents because they (and I) would have said I was dreaming.

'But it is only these last years I realise that these horrible, thin, wizened, toothless, spikey, grey-haired and some young, ill-fed people were actually in my bedroom which was built on to the Elizabethan part of the old farmhouse.

'They mocked and laughed and leered at me from behind the wardrobe, the wash stand and sometimes came close to the bed. My mother bought me an iron tonic for she realised I had dark rings under my eyes.

'I was finally moved from my bedroom because she thought it might be too cold for me. I have never forgotten the people. I actually lost weight. It was a kind of torment as if something was trying to break me down.

'As a child I had the feeling when the terror stopped of being the winner as if I had conquered a kind of fear, something my mother and father could not do for me and even at this early age, there was the knowledge that I must face it myself. That was 50 years ago and it gave me a lot of strength.'

Ben was only three but was terrified by an invisible cockerel who bit his toes. His mum tried shooing it away and even offering a bit of invisible corn but Ben could still see the cockerel who continued to menace him.

Like Edmund's lion with glasses, it is no good anyone else saying that the invisible foe has gone unless the child creates a departure scenario himself. At last Ben's desperate mum got fed up of chasing an invisible cockerel round the bedroom and garden, not to mention the odd looks she was getting from the neighbours.

So she asked Ben how they could get rid of cockerel.

'Send him back where he came from,' Ben replied and Ben knew exactly where cockerel's home was, the farm park about five miles down the road. Ben devised a plan to catch the cockerel in a large bag and throw him up into the sky so he would fly home. After a couple of false starts this was accomplished to cries of, 'Off you go cockerel and don't come back!' Cockerel came back several times. But now Ben didn't mind because now he had the power to send his invisible foe away.

Ben's mum was very understanding at what was a figment of her son's imagination. Or was it?

A couple of weeks after cockerel's final departure, Ben and his mother went to the farm park. Ben rushed over to the enclosure where the hens and cockerels were and picked out a particularly malevolent-looking black cockerel. 'Hello cockerel,' he said with a delighted smile. 'It's me, Ben.'

And his mum swears the creature left the others and came over to see them.

Sometimes a child is having a negative psychic experience as focus for the family earthly problems and resolution lies not in getting rid of the child's invisible foe but in resolving the underlying conflicts. Often then the foe will disappear as if by magic.

Marian told me the following story of a little girl called Sarah who was four and a half years old and lived in Frome in Somerset. Sarah was her friend Gill's daughter. Sarah's dad walked out of the family home and left the area after years of tension. Shortly afterwards Gill and Sarah were rehoused by the local council in a house that was vacant because of the death of the 80-year-old man who had lived there.

Then Sarah started seeing an old man. He used to sit on a chair in her bedroom. It wasn't the presence that frightened Sarah but his refusal to respond to her when she spoke. Her grandparents were the first to hear of Sarah's 'old man' and they checked with neighbours only to find Sarah's description of the old man tallied exactly with that of the previous tenant.

Visits to doctors followed but to no avail till at last they contacted a psychotherapist who was sympathetic to alternative ideas. The psychotherapist advised Gill that Sarah should have plenty of opportunities to talk about the old man and her fears and be reassured that she was special and the old man only wanted to be sure that the new family was looking after the house he had lived in and loved for most of his life.

Marian gave the family a copy of the earlier version of this book which confirmed that lots of other families had similar experiences especially in times of trouble and that they weren't bad or mad or odd and she says that the whole family used it as a basis to talk things over.

The old man's visits got less maybe as a result of bringing all the tensions out in the open and stopped completely once Sarah started school. There certainly was a psychological element but the experience can't be dismissed as imagination because the old man Sarah saw was the old man who had lived there.

The links between psychic and psychological are very complex but certainly from the experiences I've come across it seems as if the resolution or at least recognition of earthly problems does help to get rid of negative psychic experiences. Annette's phantom foe was not an imaginary friend but one who had caused problems while she was alive. Annette Monshing is a mother of two and lives in Myrtleford in Victoria, Australia. She still sees her childhood friend Lee who was killed in a road accident.

Both Annette and Lee were partially deaf and so they always enjoyed a special form of non-verbal communication that can be more powerful in some ways than words.

Annette wrote to me: 'Lee died from massive head injuries after she went through the windscreen of a car. I went to school with her. One morning not long after her death I looked in my mirror and I could see Lee's face. She was wearing her very sarcastic expression. When Lee was alive she could be overpowering.

'She would look into my eyes and you could see the determination in hers. To us eye-contact was a different way of talking. About six months before her death I found if you blinked it broke the spell and she hated that because she always wanted to be top dog.

'I suppose with Lee I'd always thought she could do better than me, talk more, speak clearer and act in a more adult way. Lee was always carefree and lived it up. But two weeks before she died she had enrolled as a nurse for old people which was her greatest ambition and seemed to be settling down.

'I've seen Lee in the mirror several times since she died, her face over mine as though she was trying to take me over. It's over a year now and I know it would be so easy for me to let her spirit in my body but I know her too well. I wouldn't be strong enough to control her.'

The fears of a small child can be fixed in the strangest ways upon a particular place. Often the stairs seem to be particularly frightening. When Sue was very small, she lived in Poole in Dorset and can remember feeling a presence on the landing whenever she went upstairs. 'It used to chase me down the stairs and I was terrified. It went on until my father painted the stairs white. It was originally brown varnish.'

One explanation for night terrors given by psychologists is that they might be 'eidetic images', pictures which are so vivid in a child's mind that he projects them into his surroundings like a cinema projector throws images on to a screen.

Experiments have been carried out in which a child is shown a picture which is then removed. Some children have the ability to point out details as though the absent picture was still there. It was said that between 30 and 90 per cent of children possessed this ability, though recent tests have put the figure as low as seven per cent. Often the child cannot understand why the adult cannot see what he is seeing.

Is the child in some way taking pictures from his imagination, a book or a television programme and unconsciously projecting them against his bedroom wall at night? Would this explain the case of Jane who told me: 'When I was a small child of about two and a half, we were living on a new council estate in Cardiff that had been built on a bomb site. I was lying in bed and I was convinced I could see a face on the wall (the same colour as the plaster, but with bright red lips).

'It was like the Queen's profile on a stamp or a cameo. I remember being absolutely terrified at the time of what the family referred to in later years as "my Lady Hoo-Hoo" which was what I must have called her when I tried to explain.'

Richard Coss, a psychologist at the University of

California interviewed 200 children aged three to four about their night terrors and discovered that more than half the girls feared monsters who came from under the bed while two thirds of boys feared things on either side of them such as outside windows and in cupboards.

He believes that the difference may be due to programming from a time in our evolutionary past when women spent more time in trees. Scientists have suggested that the lighter form and more flexible feet of females were better suited to life in trees. So it would follow they might be genetically programmed to be afraid of attacks from predators below.

Dr Coss cited a further study done with 492 adults. Sixty four per cent of males remembered terrors associated with locations at the side of them whereas the common factor with many women was again the thing under the bed.

He's now planning to create a miniature scene complete with caves and trees to ask children where they would feel safest. He comments: 'Children do actually think that they might be killed at night whether it is by an alligator, ghost, witch or dinosaur.'

Occasionally an object can seem to become a focus for the person it belonged to and in the case of Tracey's son Alex, his contact with Grandad's Indian statue was more frightening for the adults involved. Tracey told me: 'Alex is now three. We have an Indian statue that my Dad brought back after the war. We've always kept the statue out of reach so it won't get broken.

'Since Alex was a baby and able to talk he's always talked to the statue. Sometimes he's been standing in front of it crying but often he'll be laughing away as he chats. Alex was only three months old when my dad died so he never really knew him.

'I've asked Alex who he was talking to on several occasions but he wouldn't answer. At last my husband got worried and put the statue upstairs out of sight. But Alex would simply stand at the bottom of the stairs behind his stair-gate talking up the stairs. So I brought it down again as there didn't seem any point.'

I suggested to Tracey maybe Alex was chatting to Grandad whom he could see behind or near the statue. I said that if Alex did get worried about the statue the family could help him to feel he was in control and then maybe get rid of the statue.

But apart from the odd tear which we all have in earthly conversations the statue wasn't causing any problems. Most children naturally stop such contact in their own time if they are not made to feel they are silly or doing something frightening and above all mum and dad are on hand to sort out fears earthly or otherwise.

Jane who lives in Portsmouth told me: 'The other day my young daughter Rosa was sitting on my lap in her bedroom looking up at the ceiling. Suddenly a huge beam came over her face and she put her hand above her head and started waving for all she was worth. She called out, "Man, man", and for about five minutes sat there smiling and waving.

'Then she put her hand high above her head in a last goodbye and lost interest as though he had gone. She wasn't in the least perturbed.'

Perhaps Jane's calm approach helped Rosa not to be

afraid. Yet even in the calmest environment young children can have fears especially as night falls for fantasy and reality aren't sharply divided and whether psychic or psychological such terrors can best be handled by the reassurance and presence of parents.

If your children want a light on or to snuggle in with you when they have a bad nightmare blow the experts and follow your instincts. You'll know the difference between real fears and a try-on. Of course we would not let our children watch scary videos or let them go to bed with angry words ringing in their ears.

But the world can be a frightening place and when our own personal bogeyman comes to call whether we are seven or seventy we occasionally need other people to keep watch with us till morning comes.

Shirley, a medium, now blames her night terrors not on a psychological cause but definitely on the supernatural. She says that when she was little she was plagued by people in her bedroom — men, women and children — that no one else could see and would hide under her bedclothes with fear. Now she says she realises that it was the beginning of her psychic powers.

She remembers when she was about five seeing an old lady with black robes sitting on her bed and an old man who used to stand in the corner. She was the middle child of five and used to frighten the others so much that, eventually she was put in a bedroom on her own.

Her mother used to get very cross with her for 'talking such nonsense' and smacked her so she learned to keep quiet about what she saw. She says she now knows that her father was psychic, but he kept quiet about it then as her mother was a very dominant woman.

When she was five she used to sit on the step after about six o'clock if her mum was out, as she was too frightened to go in because of all the 'people' inside.

She thinks it is sad if children do see things and like her did not have her fears explained. 'If you are afraid of your psychic awareness,' she says, 'your imagination will conjure up all sorts of horrid things.'

With her own children, she was very careful to protect them and show them there was nothing to be afraid of while at the same time encouraging them to have lots of real friends and interests.

Teenagers' growing intellectual abilities do not necessarily make them less vulnerable to frightening experiences. The teenager knows more of the dark side of life than a young child, and yet does not have the reassurance that wise adults can put it all right. They see the questions and cannot find the answers.

Gina was brought up in a household where her father was Muslim and mother Christian. At the age of 16, she wrote: 'I remember as a child talking to God quite frequently because I was afraid of my parents because they hit me. I found God was the only person I could talk to for help and it was quite comforting to know or believe there was someone there to help and look after me. I think this belief enabled me to have contact with a power.

'Ever since that day, I have seen presences in the house. I have had powers shout my name so piercing in my head I have become very afraid.

'I cannot contain these powers and I cannot force them to do anything for me or for anyone. I have written to

164

clairvoyants and they have told me I have the gift which will develop. I tried to tell my mother. She said "yes, dear" and never took it further.'

Gina's voices may well represent many underlying fears about her life in a mixed culture family where she feels torn apart emotionally. What is worrying is that sensitive teenagers can be egged on by postal clairvoyants, some of whom may have no interest except in making money.

Graham is an intelligent, very sensitive only child. When he was 15, he began to feel threatened by ghosts in his comfortable suburban home. One, he said, was under the stairs and grabbed him. 'I was facing towards the main hall with my eyes shut. I felt him pull my shoulders and twist me. Another time, he tried to pull me into the cupboard. I saw him from the top of his forehead to the mouthline. He had a wispy beard, thin wire-framed glasses, long nose and a kind face.

'One Friday recently, I was studying in my bedroom. Mum was at work. I glanced up at the door and saw a man standing there. As soon as I blinked. He was gone. He had a moustache, black beard and a Homburg hat, with black band. He wore a long woollen trench coat. Now when I'm in the house on my own and hear the creak on the stairs. I get really freaked out.'

Unlike Gina, Graham is not isolated with his fears. Although his father is away a great deal with his job and is not particularly enthusiastic about psychic matters, his mother is not only sympathetic, but says she also feels the presences in the house.

Five months later, I asked Graham what was happening

to his ghosts and if he was still freaked out. 'I still see things out of the corner of my eye,' he said. 'I think I saw my grandad who had recently died. Now it's all under control. I say a prayer when I go to bed. Then I visualise myself wrapped completely in a bandage, like a mummy, and I am safe until morning.'

To those who have not been haunted or have not felt the terror of being haunted, such precautions may seem like sprinkling the oofle dust to keep the elephants out of your bedroom. ('But there aren't any elephants within a hundred miles of here,' runs the old joke. 'Yes,' says the oofle dust user, 'effective stuff isn't it.')

But is our rational world any saner? The French novelist, Romain Gary, once wrote that people were fools for thinking Don Quixote mad because he lived in a world populated by giants and ogres. It was Sancho Panza who was mad, he said, for not seeing what monsters there really were in life.

Chapter Ten

Dealings With The Dark Side

'**A**T THE MOMENT I've got four poltergeists on the go. There's a sudden run on them, I had none the previous three months. In one of the worst cases, a woman had been dabbling in Satanism. She had given it up, but not renounced it. She had her kids baptised and they brought home the baptism candles. The candlesticks flew across the room and things started to happen. I was called in and I found it could read my mind.'

I was lucky that, despite his workload , the Reverend Tom Willis, a Church of England vicar in Yorkshire could spare some time to talk to me. As well as looking after two churches he is one of 10 priests in the diocese of York who have been appointed to deal with cases of the occult disturbances. 'The old word for us is exorcists, but I don't like using that word as it conjures up an image of black cloaks and flames coming out of my fingers,' he says.

Married with five children, he has been involved with the paranormal for more than 20 years. 'There were a lot of problems in the 1960s. People thought I was a nut when I said that the occult was a growing problem. Then the flood came and the Samaritans started to ring up the C of E regularly, saying "We don't know what to do". I had done talks on whether the paranormal existed but I had no real training.

'But they said, "Ask Tom Willis, he knows about that sort of thing".

' I didn't have much experience, but I was thrown into the front line and I used to go out with the Samaritans. I also used to get called out by the police.

'The work I do is part of the healing ministry. I try to bring peace to a place or to people. Sometimes I have to deal with a house. Sometimes what I have to deal with is related to the people involved.'

We had discussed benign ghosts (his comments and stories on these have been recorded in the chapter on ghostly grandparents) but I was also interested, in the light of some stories I had been told, in the darker side of his work.

Did he believe that in this day and age evil spirits could possess young children?

'If people themselves believe they are possessed, then it may well be a psychological case. But some people do seem to have evil around them and may display weird behaviour.

'I have laid my hands and asked for the evil to depart. Even if it is not a case of evil, it may work on spiritual or psychological level. I know a Roman Catholic priest, a down-to-earth, likeable, Irish beer-drinking priest who was called to a case of possession in a teenager.

'He was very dubious till he saw her lying rigid and then taking off four or five inches off the floor. He realised something serious was going on and commanded evil to depart.'

Did he believe in evil as a real living force that could think and act? I asked. 'There is a fascination with evil at a subconscious level. No one talks about the possibility that evil may have intelligence — it is considered twee , like believing in fairies — to regard evil in that way. But the minute war is gone from one part of the planet, it pops up in another. Disease, too, is eradicated but another takes its place.

'Evil is a blob that you clear from one place and it appears in another.'

He agreed that children were possibly more psychic than adults. 'They lose this power as they get older. I suppose it is because logical processes take over. I have known cases where the child is the first in the family to witness a haunting.

As the Reverend Willis said in the earlier chapter, the Church has no objections when grandparents want to return briefly from the dead to visit a new grandchild.

But he warns strongly against dabbling with the occult for fear that what is called up might not be what was asked for. The ouija board, he says, has a strong fascination for children.

'I speak to children in secondary schools and warn them off the ouija board. I recently asked 100 fourth and fifth year kids, 14 and 15-year-olds, how many of them had played with ouija boards. Two thirds put up their hands, there were less girls than boys. The girls were more interested in the astrological side.

'The teacher gasped at the sea of hands that went up. It is partly a craze of that particular age group.'

Before speaking to the Reverend Willis I had already been told about the dramatic and horrifying effects of the ouija board on an impressionable child's mind. A few days before a mother had told me that when her daughter was about 12, she and some of her friends had been playing with a ouija board in the school cloakroom at lunchtime after she found a book in the school library about it.

The daughter believes she picked up a spirit because she started to be haunted by an oldish man.

'He used to sit on her dressing table,' said Pat, her mother. 'He followed her all the time. He used to just sit there watching her. It was horrifying.' Things got so bad one night when Pat's husband was at work that Pat rang their Catholic priest but he was out.

'My daughter was completely hysterical. I talked to her to calm her and we sprinkled holy water round her room. After that, it seemed to quieten down. I made her promise never to fool around with a ouija board again.'

Ashi went to an exclusive convent school in the Home Counties and had dabbled with the ouija board from the age of 14 during lunch-time break in the classroom. When Ashi was 16, she and her best friend Ally were playing with the board and as Ashi told me:

'It was a time when school friendships are the centre of your world and you can't imagine it being otherwise. So

Ally asked the glass, "Will Ashi and I always be friends?"

' "No."

' "Why not?"

' "Dead. Car."

'Ally was very upset and we stopped doing the ouija after that. But six months later almost to the day Ally was killed in a car crash.'

The activities of poltergeists, the noisy ghosts who are alleged to cause so much disruption in houses, are often linked with children.

'The current theory on poltergeists is that some electrical force comes from a living person who is repressing great anger,' the Reverend Willis told me.

'From one, I got the biggest electric shock I have had in my life. It knocked me off my feet. The force went through the fifteen-year-old son, but had been lessened by passing through me, but he still crumpled up. By the time, it reached the mum, she said, "Ouch! What was that?"

'I have had objects flying about while I stood in the midst. I had read about this, but never believed it till I saw it. There was a dog ornament on one mantelpiece where the objects kept moving, a clock and ashtray. "The dog's gone again," said the householder.

'I was sitting there and heard a clunk in the kitchen. All the doors were closed. "Don't move," I said and I went into the kitchen.

'There was the dog ornament, gone clean through the wall.

'I consulted a physicist at Hull University. "Is it possible for objects to move through brick walls?" I asked him.

' "According to the quantum mechanical tunnel theory, if it went at the speed of light, there would be no problem. But it's not provable since you can't hurl objects at the speed of light!" he said.'

Poltergeist activity can be less spectacular but still frightening for those involved. Jill, now married and with a family of her own, told me this incident from her childhood.

'I was always scared of the back bedroom where I used to sleep. We moved to the house when I was 11. The main thing I noticed was that it was always freezing in there. I had a friend to stay not long after we moved. We had single beds quite a way apart.

'I woke up in the night and the bed was shaking. I got up and it carried on shaking. My friend woke up too and her bed was shaking. She remembered it years later. I told my parents and they said, "It's because we live near the railway".

'But we were about half a mile from the track which was on the other side of the house. It was the only time it happened in the six years we were at the house and it didn't happen in my friend's house and she lived next door.

'When I was 13 or 14, I started to have a dream about an upside down cross. We weren't a religious family and never went to church. I was horrified to be told by my friends that it was to do with the devil. Not long after I had an awful vision of the devil He had huge horns like a ram and a horrible face. His face was dark and half ram, half human.

'I don't believe in the devil now, but I had no doubt then. I think I said a prayer. I felt a physical force He was trying to crush me. I was absolutely terrified. It lasted 10 or 15 seconds I suppose, but it was like eternity.

'My parents took no notice. They always said it was my imagination, They were strong people who did not show emotion.' She went to a doctor for help and he advised her to recite the Lord's Prayer.

Janet, who lives in Bracknell, is now in her late thirties but can still recall the demon that terrified her as a teenager.

She described her experience: 'When I was about sixteen I had an experience that frightened the life out of me. I woke to find a heaving weight on my chest choking the life from my body. The room was freezing. I could see the dent on the bed this invisible force was making and I was fighting to breathe as it grasped me and pressed my neck till I thought I would suffocate from my veins. At last it went suddenly, leaving me shaking and exhausted.

'This happened on two occasions. The second time I said the Lord's Prayer and the fiend as I thought of it never came back.'

But it is not only girls who confront such forces in adolescence. Anna, an experienced religious education teacher said that a fifteen-year-old boy in her class confided in her that when he looked in the mirror he saw the face of the devil over his shoulder.

'He was frightened as he couldn't talk to his parents about it and asked me what he should do. I suggested he might think of something good and substitute it for the bad thing that was terrifying him. I didn't know how else to help. It seemed to work but I wondered if he had other problems he felt he couldn't share.'

There have been cases of poltergeist phenomena being produced by blatant fraud. Dr Hans Bender, a German parapsychologist, videotaped a little girl supposedly the victim of poltergeist activity, leaping out of bed, slinging an ornament, hopping back into bed and shouting 'Help, mum'. But most cases are not funny.

More disturbing, to my mind, is the case of an eight-year-old boy in a town in southern England who was rejected by his foster-parents because he was blamed for bringing a poltergeist upon them. I will call the child concerned Kenny as he will now be reaching manhood and has settled with new foster-parents so there is little point in identifying him and possibly reviving painful memories for all concerned. Kenny's first foster mother suffered from a progressive illness and the boy was diagnosed as educationally backward, which is some-times regarded as a significant factor in poltergeist cases (or it may be that so-called retarded children are less able to explain what really happened).

There was considerable disturbance in the house, book-cases spilling, china smashed and a medium called in by the social worker identified the presence of a boy called Don who said he played with Kenny in the garden.

The foster father said that the lad did say he was playing with a boy called Don who had a bicycle when in fact there was apparently no one there with him (though as we have seen an imaginary friend is not at all unusual). This Don was linked by the medium with a young down-and-out who had died in the area.

A newspaper reporter did point out at the time that there was a real Don with a bicycle who lived nearby whom Kenny sometimes played with. But this was ignored and by the time the police and priests had said their piece and the neighbours had offered their words of wisdom, it was only left for the friendly neighbourhood self-styled white witch to bring the situation to boiling point by pinpointing 'the malevolent force' to the unfortunate boy, apparently because of some unspecified early trauma in his life.

She felt that if he was removed everything would be fine. So the lad was removed and the activity ceased (though apparently nothing occurred at his new home).

Whatever the, psychic truth of events, it seems a sad indictment that it should be the child, perhaps most in need of help, who was seen as the cause and was the one to suffer.

It is perhaps dangerous to view a child's psychic experiences, bad or otherwise as emanating from the child in isolation. They are a part of the whole family situation and the removal of one member can be a false and particularly sad solution.

Peter King, president of the Reading National Spiritualist Church considers that the medium could not have been a responsible one or she would have tried to enlist the help of the spirits and talk to the poltergeist.

Phil is now a teenager but can still recall the haunted home of his childhood. The trouble began when his mother remarried and his new step-father moved in.

Phil explained: 'Every night we could hear a creaking noise coming from the loft. Mum thought it might be wind but the noise happened even when there was no wind. My step-dad went into the loft and found an old chair rocking by itself. He saw a white figure move across the window.

'Then when we were having dinner, plates would start being thrown around by themselves. Mum was really scared so she got the local vicar in. He came quite a few times and said it would be all right but after he went the noises would always come back.

'We started to sleep downstairs because it was so scary. At last my stepdad got the rocking chair from the loft. I was hiding under the covers but the chair flew out of his hands and threw my step-dad on to my bed. The chair landed on me and really hurt me.

'My step-dad threw the chair on to a bonfire but it did no good. Things kept flying round and breaking so in the end we moved out of the house. But I am now living with foster parents because my step-dad used to hurt me.'

Jane is a computer analyst in her early thirties. She grew up in a cottage in North Warwickshire with her mum, dad and elder sister. When Jane was eleven she woke one night and saw an old man sitting on the end of her bed but she wasn't frightened. She smiled at him and he smiled back. The old man had a cap, a stick and piercing blue eyes.

Unusually, Jane's parents didn't laugh but looked shocked when she described the old man though they wouldn't say why. It wasn't till years later Jane found out she had seen the previous owner of the house who had died in her room. Her parents had been experiencing problems in their marriage for some time and there had been many late-night arguments.

Jane's sister spent a lot of time away from the family so Jane felt very isolated with the family troubles. Indeed when she sat at breakfast if there was an unhappy atmosphere plates and ornaments would start to move. Her parents accused her of playing tricks but as their marriage deteriorated Jane became even more frightened.

One evening when everyone was in the kitchen they heard footsteps coming downstairs. Jane had heard footsteps in the middle of the night when she was younger but her parents had told her she was dreaming. This time even her dad was scared and it was the first time the family admitted that there might be something haunting them.

In spite of this, Jane's parents took her to different psychiatrists and therapists who all suggested she was trying to punish her parents by playing tricks on them. Jane became more and more nervous and anorexic and her experiences were explained as a symptom of her eating problems.

But the paranormal activity did not stop until Jane's mother left home. Years later Jane's mother still will not talk about what happened. Jane still has a problem with food.

Sometimes, it would seem, the poltergeist is not malevolent, but unhappy and taking out his feelings on the more vulnerable members of the family, the children. Lilian, a psychic counsellor, told me about a family with four children, who believed they were being persecuted by a poltergeist.

The mother, a nurse, insisted that their house was haunted by a small thing which was quite vicious, although the creature was not malevolent towards her personally.

Her husband knew of the presence, but believed that the less said about it, the better.

Two of the children, the eldest and the youngest were terrified of the creature and would not sleep in a particular bedroom because they said it was there. Lilian says that when she went to the house, she felt the presence was eluding her. She stayed in the bedroom with it, but it went off into a corner.

However, as Lilian began chatting to the mother, she says she felt the small thing attach itself to the woman: it seemed to be a small boy who could neither see, hear, nor speak and its only anchor of security was the mother. Lilian asked the mother if she had ever known a child like that.

The mother recognised it as her sister's child who had lived in the house and slept in the bedroom that the children were afraid of. The child had died when he was about two but her sister had shown him very little affection and it had been left to her alone to show him any affection.

Lilian said the child was jealous of the children living in the house who had usurped 'his mum' and were taking up her attention.

So Lilian tried to contact the spirit of her own dead mother to come and look after the child. But Lilian's mother was out of reach and the ghost child was determined to stay. Eventually Lilian said: 'Look I can't get rid of it for you, But now you know who it is, do you really want it to go?'

The mother decided 'no' and the little deaf, dumb, blind spirit remained in residence, but proved much more co-operative from then on.

Vivien Greene, who encountered her first ghost when she was quite young, told me that in later life, while she was on holiday, she came across a deeply distressed ghost child.

'When I was in Tenerife on holiday with my young son, we were staying in a hotel run by a German refugee. The old hotel has since been entirely destroyed and replaced by a fifteen storey building. It was soon after the war. There were two rooms built out over a covered in jetty. The water would be washing about underneath and you could see it through the cracks. There was one big room and one small. My son, Francis, was going to sleep in the little room but I knew I could not let him sleep in there because I had the most dreadful feeling about it. So I used that room instead.

'During the night I saw an apparition of a decaying church and cemetery with a wicked child fiend running up and down. There were railings between us. ''I will pray for you,'' I said but I was told I was not good enough to help him.

'Francis was about eight at the time. We changed bedrooms to another part of the hotel the next night. I did not tell the owner why because he had to do everything and was rushed off his feet.'

Jealousy was also a factor with what was described as a young female poltergeist who frightened Moira and attacked her sister. In this case it was the family who moved on after many years of haunting.

The ghost was alleged to be one of grandad's old flames from the war who got very annoyed of anyone else getting his attention, even his granddaughters of whom he was very fond.

Moira tells how when she was four years old she and her baby sister and mother and father moved to a big old house which they shared with her grandfather and grandmother

'Even then I sensed something strange about the house and used to lie awake at night listening to the strange noises from the landing. I used to cry because of the sounds outside my door. But no one ever appeared.

'When I was about seven, the noises got too close for comfort and I locked myself in the toilet for about two hours till mum came and took me on a tour of the house to prove that nothing was there.

'One night, when I was at secondary school, I was sitting on the floor in my grandad's lounge when suddenly a wall light switched itself off and then on and off again. He laughed and said: "She's here again". Recently he had been seeing a young girl about 20 walking behind him. Sometimes she was just a white outline and sometimes she looked like flesh and blood. I pressured him for more details, but he would not talk about her much. I am certain no one else knew.

'When my sister was 11, she woke up screaming one night. She said a girl had come into her room, hurt her and then come into my room.

'One night, when I was about 14, I woke up and could not sleep. Someone was walking up the stairs. I began to panic .Burglaries were common in our area. Something moved across to my sister's room and I heard paper being thrown everywhere, then the books.

'I thought she must be sleepwalking. I screamed to mum but when she went into Lorna's room everything was in its place.

'A couple of months later, my mum, sister and I moved out, as my mum and dad had agreed to a divorce. We moved into a flat and nan and grandad sold the house. A medium told my grandad that the young woman had been a nurse who had helped him during the war and had fallen for him. Grandad had lost a leg.'

Once Moira discovered her grandad's ghost, it explained her own earlier 'spooky experiences'. The girl who attacked her sister fitted in, as did the apparent ransacking of her sister's room. Not long after, the family split up which would suggest that there was great underlying tension in the family.

Did the family members, involved in the marital upheaval that could well have been simmering for years, need a ghost to make sense of the tensions and stresses they did not understand.

In family therapy, it is accepted that a 'problem' does not just belong to an individual or a couple, but is rooted in the family. Where one part of the family is distorted, the rest of the family will have to change shape correspondingly. Where three generations are involved, the problem is even more complex.

Was this a 'family haunting' that fitted in with the medium's explanation, or was the young nurse still pining after her lost love and jealous of the affection the old man showed to his little granddaughters?

A strong Christian faith cannot always provide protection against apparent manifestations of evil. It may be that they provide even more tempting targets for such forces.

Andrea wrote: 'When I was 17, I had an experience during Lent. Being the regular church organist/piano player, I was asked to play for four consecutive Tuesday evenings. On the second, before starting the service, I sat at the piano rehearsing a few hymns with the congregation in the church hall where the service was being held.

'Upon practising the last hymn, I casually peered over to the front doors — I presume I was expecting to see any late arrivals — but a kind of woman was staring in at me, expressionless with no features, dead, white flesh with a black scarf of some kind which went all round her head. I went dizzy and my heart beat fast, but I just couldn't tear my eyes away from it. I looked away but had to look again and finally let out a loud gasp. Everyone shut up suddenly and the vicar asked what was wrong.

'For some unknown reason, I said I thought I'd seen my dead grandmother. Why I said that I don't know, but what I'd seen was unexplainable. During the peace, the vicar's wife came over to comfort me and said that Satan tries to destroy church services. My playing the piano made me a target.

'Last Sunday evening, at service again, I suddenly sensed a frightening sensation during the start of the service. I didn't dare turn round to the front doors, but I asked the vicar to pray and he cleared the church hall and asked whatever was bad to go. After that I felt a lot better.'

Whether Andrea did see the devil or a manifestation of her fears of being possessed we do not know. A sense of powerlessness, felt by teenagers, can be as strong as a fear of being possessed.

Are perhaps, poltergeist and demons saying something about these fears in the growing child and indeed his family? We may think we see demons or are being attacked by poltergeists when what we are perhaps saying is 'I feel attacked by what is going on'.

Equally, psychic experiences can trigger a psychological reaction. The relationship is so complex it requires greater investigation.

On the positive side, Eileen Orford of the Tavistock Clinic, says: 'We need ways of thinking about our fears. They are better in the form of monsters than in the unconscious. At least as monsters they are not a nameless dread.'

Of course it can be Mum herself who is conjuring up the phantoms. Carolyn whom I met at a playgroup in Woodley near Reading told me her gran was a medium: 'One night when Mum was little my nan was reading her a story. Suddenly one of the dining room chairs tipped up. Nan was delighted. ''Tap once for yes and twice for no,'' Nan told the chair and she and the chair entered into a fascinating conversation.

'Mum was absolutely petrified and fled for her life but Nan didn't even notice.'

Chapter Eleven

Changelings

NOTHING seems more innocent and beautiful than a sleeping new-born child. But imagine if you were to pick up that child and it suddenly opened its eyes, smiled to reveal a full row of teeth and said: 'I am very small but my teeth are very sharp.'

That scenario — so terrifying because of the contrast between innocence and malevolence — occurs in John Steinbeck's novel, *The Long Valley* and introduces a character to be found in folklore all over Europe: the changeling.

The legends describe the changeling as a wizened, misshapened baby, hairy and with a monstrous head, which is left in the cradle as a substitute for a human child snatched by the fairies or underground elves. It is said to eat ravenously but never grow (or if it grows to be horribly deformed) and to cry continually. The fairies or sprites are said to desire human babies for their tender flesh and to carry them off to fairyland where they are made much of.

Folklore offers various remedies: to make the every-crying changeling laugh or to trick it into revealing its true age. The story of the soldier and the egg exists in various versions in many parts of the country. A soldier returns home from the wars to find his younger brother still in the cradle after some 20 years. The mother has not caught on yet that there's anything amiss ('He's still a growing lad, dear') but the soldier has knocked around a bit and has his suspicions. So he empties an eggshell, fills it with water and begins heating it over a fire which amuses the changeling enough for it to laugh out loud and say: 'Old, old I am but in all my years I have never seen a soldier brewing beer in an eggshell.'

The deception now revealed, the soldier feels free to attack the changeling with a whip and, by magic, it vanishes and the long lost brother, now a grown man is restored to the family. According to some versions he is a little bit peeved at the reunion because in fairyland where he had been imprisoned for all those years he lived the life of Reilly and knows that conditions at home might be a little more basic.

Other versions of the tale neglect the egg brewing and go straight into the whipping option at which point the fairy or elf who carried out the substitution appears, crying: 'Do not attack my child for I never did yours any harm,' and returns the missing baby.

Victor Hugo used a variant of the changeling legend in *The Hunchback of Notre Dame* where the baby Quasimodo, the hideous but immensely strong cripple, is swapped for the beautiful Esmeralda. But here the substitution is carried out by gypsies not fairies.

As the changeling is so widespread in folklore, it is interesting to speculate on what basis there could be for it in reality. Was it the way for parents in less enlightened times than ours to come to terms with deformed or handicapped children? I asked a doctor with an interest in paranormal experiences about the medical aspects.

'The description of a changeling is not identifiable as a particular syndrome,' he said, 'rather a series of deformities that separately or together would mark a child as odd. There are children who look odd from the moment they are born and come to look stranger. When parents have a child that looks strange, one acceptable hypothesis in times past was that the devil had got into the child somehow.

'Many conditions — cretinism or gargoylism for example — that can give rise to a bizarre and unattractive appearance. Dietary shortages in times past can explain much of the lack of growth, especially in poor families. A large head can of course be linked in some cases with hydrocephalus. In those days, a high proportion of children failed to thrive and infant mortality was as high as 50 to 60 per cent.

'The changeling explanation was much more convenient explanation for unfortunate parents who produced a monster and made it more acceptable to them. Until the last 50 or 60 years only strong, healthy children survived.'

For the child taken to be a changeling, life could be hard, especially if the parents decided to use the whipping method. In 1843 The West Briton newspaper reported the case of a J Trevelyan of Penzance who was charged with ill-treating one of his children. The child was said to have been regularly beaten by the parents and the servants and from 15 months old had been left to live outside. The parents defence was that he was not their child but a changeling and the case against them was dismissed (this case is quoted in The Folklore of Cornwall, by Tony Deane and Tony Shaw, published by Batsford).

'You have to remember that a century and a half ago,' the doctor told me, 'the railway had only just broken through to Cornwall and until then it had been virtually cut off. When Wesley went there in the 1780s he found a land rife with paganism and folklore. Cornwall at that time was appallingly backward with gross poverty, great ignorance and conditions that horrified Wesley.'

Times may have improved but the problem lingers of the child who does not quite fit in with the family, the 'Cinderella' who can be of either sex.

'As a doctor one sees some women who do not like one of their children and feel very guilty about this. In the past, the hypothesis that the Devil was in the child made it easier for them to accept this situation. When people used to have a number of children, anything up to a dozen, this was not uncommon: the unloved child who was blamed for everything.'

If one old belief has retreated, another surrounding children has managed to grow in strength: possession by demonic forces. Perhaps the flames of this belief have been fanned by films like *The Exorcist,* (child possession), *Rosemary's Baby* (a child sired by Satan), *The Omen* (a changeling) and the B-Movies that followed trying to cash in on the vogue for tales of Satanic children. One disturbing film was based on Ray Bradbury's story, *The Baby*, in which a baby is born with a mature mind and murderously attacks its parents for daring to bring it into the world away from the peace and quiet of the womb.

Hollywood is now conditioning us to think of possession in terms of spectacular special effects. However, it can be more subtle in real life, although none the less unnerving for the parent who believes that his or her child may be possessed.

When I discussed Louise's story with her she struck me as a very pleasant, rational woman. She feared that her son, Edmund, had been possessed even before his birth.

She believes this 'thing' entered Edmund in Cornwall where he was conceived. 'I had an overwhelming desire to go to Cornwall for most of my childhood and adult life. I believe that the being somehow got me to Cornwall so it could be born again through my son. It is an area of enormous fascination for me. The year before Edmund was conceived, we were staying on the south-west side of Bodmin Moor, camping beside a river bank. I experienced an overwhelming desire to go along the river bank early in the morning. I felt as if I could see lots of figures — not as distinct persons but as indistinct shadows ——lots of figures, maybe a hundred. I felt as if they were standing along the banks of the river welcoming me.'

At the time Louise contacted me, in 1989, Edmund was eight. 'From the beginning, he was always very different. Sometimes I would look at him and it was as if his face was not his face any more. During my elder son's pregnancy and birth I felt calm and happy.

'But Edmund's pregnancy was very different, I felt very depressed and worried, though I felt it was inevitable he would be born. He was not planned, but he had to come.

'Edmund's pregnancy closely followed a nervous breakdown and a serious illness. All I remember about the pregnancy is feeling thoroughly exhausted and physically ill.'

Louise believes that a message from Edmund altered her carefully laid birth plans. It was agreed by the midwife that Louise should give again give birth in a squatting position. All was going well till the final examination in labour when Louise was lying prone on the bed. 'Suddenly I felt taken over, that I had lost the power to be me. I felt the child and had to lie prone. The midwife and Tony tried to haul me up the bed so I could squat as planned to give birth.

'But I refused. It was not like with Harry, my elder son. I felt I had no choice. When Edmund was born, the cord was wound tightly round his neck. The midwife said if I had given birth in any other position except prone, he would most likely have died.'

Everything that could, went wrong. Illness meant her husband could not work for a long time, problems with their house had them camping in one room. 'I felt so swept along and taken over.'

'Somehow in some strange way, I've always felt Edmund to have a will so strong that any desires of mine or anyone else's were overridden. Could that will have manifested itself even then?

'From the first he was a very difficult baby. My first very brief reaction was sheer annoyance at his maleness as I had very much wanted a girl, but literally only for a second. Then I fell in love with him.

'But his eyes were peculiar. They seemed unlike a baby's eyes. I remember sitting up in bed with him propped up on my knees and he gazed around the room very slowly and calmly. Calculating is the way I've always described it, but how can a baby of only a few hours look calculating? I phoned my mum soon afterwards. I wanted to say "Help, I've had a strange baby," but I didn't because I never could have explained why I found him strange. Edmund looked like a little old man when he was born. People would say you would not know he was a child.'

Louise was very ill again and her husband had to take on a lot of the care for Edmund during the next few years. As he grew up, Louise says, Edmund would say, 'I don't know what makes me be like that,' when he seemed to be malevolent.

'When Edmund was what we described as hyped up, which could be generated by a number of things including some foods, watching television or a computer screen, over-excitement, or some kinds of fluorescent lighting, he would seem physically changed as if his body became like an old man. His skin felt strange in these moods, not firm like a child's and would go yellowy-whitey in colour. His voice would become loud and strident and he'd use foul, abusive language. And he would make a hideous face, (which always reminded me of a gargoyle) and scrunch his hands up and hold them rigidly beside his ears. His eyes would roll up and he would leer.

'It always made me feel terrible and I couldn't fathom

why he was behaving like this. If people did not like him, he became worried and reacted badly. He would react badly to a person or situation that made him feel rejected. The more people he was with the more likely he was to lose control.'

She described Edmund as a gifted child with a high IQ but with many problems with conventional schooling. At eight, he was asked to leave the private school he had been attending for only a few weeks because of his disruptive behaviour — 'an evil feeling or presence which Edmund seemed to bring into the class', was how an overwrought teacher had described it.

A friend suggested Louise might take Edmund to a psychic healer he knew who had seen Edmund and felt something might be troubling him. Louise talked to the healer and Edmund went to play in the next room. 'The healer felt that Edmund was possessed by an evil spirit,' said Louise, 'and suddenly everything fitted together.

'What does it look like? How does it manifest itself?' I asked.

'I see it sitting on his shoulder,' she said and made the face I had seen on Edmund when he had almost seemed possessed many, many times in the past.

'It was quite a malevolent sort of chap, she said, who was making Edmund unhappy and didn't want to go off where he belonged. But she reckoned she could get rid of him for us.

'At the faith healing, my husband, the healer and I made a circle. The healer talked to the spirit, telling it that it was in the wrong place. 'The time has come for you to go on'.

'I felt tremendous relief and tears rolled down my

cheeks. My husband felt really drained. We did not see anything, nor did Edmund feel anything in the next room where he was playing. I felt very sad and drained. But since then, we have never seen Edmund's strange face and there has been a dramatic change. The treatment had a profoundly calming effect on him.

'The faith healer said that the being was somehow stuck. It had been waiting to attach itself to the right people who would help it on its way and knew we would eventually get rid of it. It was an incredibly stressful time for the family. Edmund was not aware of the presence. We did not tell him what we believed about the presence. He was a very nervous child and would not go into rooms, saying something would get him. Edmund always has to lie with his back to the wall, facing the room.

'We had several more treatments with the healer as she wanted to work on my relationship with him and also on him through me. She thought that Edmund had other companions who were not so closely linked and certainly not malevolent, but which ought to be removed. Edmund often wanted me to be there during his treatments and at first I saw nothing.

'But on one occasion, I was amazed to see a misty semi-transparent film or sheet lifted off his body and formed into a very tall indistinct shape beside him and then vanished — all in a few seconds. The feeling I had then was regret and sadness emanating from this figure. When the treatment finished, Edmund just got up and ran off to play as if nothing had happened.

'I ached with sorrow for my son until recently. But the change in him has been amazing. This holiday for the first time, he has gone to a holiday club at the local gymnasium with a whole range of activities and seems to be enjoying it and coping fine.'

Whatever happened at the healer's has been some sort of trigger. Helen Manning, the family therapist, agrees that there are similarities between this kind of experience and therapeutic practice. 'Any form of psychotherapy raises the individual's awareness and gives credibility, acknowledging the experience and giving value to what is said and experienced. Afterwards it is different. Awareness is raised and things can't be the same. If you acknowledge the experience, whether the child's or mother's, it enables them to make a change. It need only be something small. Exorcism is like this.'

My doctor friend commented: 'One of the great functions of all healers is to pronounce something and let people off the hook. Miracles are a fascinating subject, though they upset many rationalist doctors. If people are trapped in a disturbed and disturbing relationship and an immense authority can say, "I have removed the devil, now you may love your child," sometimes there is a breakthrough in the relationship.'

Perhaps the early traumas of Edmund's life, Louise's illnesses, the stress surrounding his pregnancy and his 'differentness' contributed to some breakdown in relationships, which the healing repaired. Or it may be argued that Edmund was possessed by some spirit in Cornwall at his conception, as Louise, an intelligent, articulate woman who is now studying for a degree in science, believes. Which ever theory is correct, the experience with the healer triggered off a dramatic improvement.

It is a fallacy that all mothers fall instantly in love with their babies. If the birth is difficult or the circumstances at home are not ideal, for example if the mother is very young and trying to bring up a baby in cramped conditions with few facilities, it is not surprising mother love can be slow to grow. But there can be tremendous guilt and anxiety which can pass on to the baby, making him difficult to feed and frequently sick or indeed if the baby is just naturally a difficult feeder, then this can make the mother feel even more inadequate.

The case of Judy is interesting because the supernatural force she encountered did not turn her against the baby but helped her to love it. 'I was 20 with a four-month-old baby,' she wrote. 'He was a sturdy child but suffered from dreadful bouts of sickness. I lived in a caravan on the moors and my husband worked nights.

'I had given the baby his bedtime feed. It was summer and the nights were light. Suddenly, he was sick everywhere. I was terrified, so I grabbed nappies and feed and set off down the lonely glen, walked up the steep hill and caught a bus to my mother's where I left the baby once the doctor had been.

'Then I made the return journey, glad to be home before dark. I was toiling up the final yards to the caravan when I heard a voice, say "Go and bring your baby back". Only lately I have wondered why this did not strike me as unusual.

'Without pausing, I turned back, fetched the baby and once again made the exhausting two and a half miles uphill. It was dark by the time I got back to the caravan. Again I heard the voice. For three days I fed the baby glucose and water only during the day and put no clothes on him and left him in the shade. On the third night, I fell asleep as usual.

'I woke later with the knowledge there was a presence in the caravan. I quickly sat up and called out, thinking my husband had come home early because he was sick. We were far away from street lights or even the reflections from the city lights below and I always kept my curtains closed. Yet plain to see next to the little cot beside the bed was a small figure, about five feet four inches tall, surrounded by a soft light. It was cowled and I saw no face. I watched unafraid. When the figure and the light faded, I lay down and knew my baby would be all right. He was never sick again. I felt no motherly love for the baby until then. He was always cared for, but I did not really love him.

'I now believe the experience was meant to form a bond and it made me feel much more responsible for the child.'

This experience appears to have acted as a trigger for a dramatic improvement in the relationship. Was it the baby's guardian who came to tell her to 'fetch your baby back' and appeared beside the cot? Whatever it was, mother and baby are doing well.

Chapter Twelve

Other Lives

ANOTHER BELIEF THAT taps the idea that children may be creatures of another dimension is that of rebirth. Although this idea is central to Hinduism and Buddhism, it is not purely an Eastern conception. Wordsworth wrote:

'Our birth is but a sleep and a forgetting,
The Soul that rises with us,our life's Star
Hath had elsewhere it's setting
And cometh from afar.'

We do not know for certain whether we have existed before but some children do seem to have strong pre-birth memories. The late Reverend Edna Rowlinson provided the following account of the experiences of Celia: ' I nursed my daughter Muriel who died when she was 28. Muriel was very patient and told me one day she wanted to dedicate her life to caring for small children if she recovered. Her sister Jean was expecting her first baby and Muriel desperately wanted to live to see the baby.

'But as the birth grew nearer Muriel got weaker. One day she woke from a light sleep and told me, "Mother, I've just seen Jean's baby. It's a dear little girl and she is very small. I'm so glad I've seen her."

'Soon afterwards Muriel died and a fortnight later Jean went into hospital telling the nurses confidently that she was having a girl. And she did give birth to Ginny, a very small but perfect infant that grew up into a lovely little girl who was loved by everyone who met her and very like her aunt in many ways.

'One day Ginny said to her mother, "Mummy, I know Aunty Muriel."

' "No dear," Jean replied, "you never knew her but you seem to know her because I have told you such a lot about her."

'But Ginny persisted. "I do know her, mummy. I have seen her really and truly. I saw her before I came to live here." '

Mothers can feel their child has lived before. Anya lived in South Africa and lost a baby daughter who was only ten weeks old. She was so devastated she vowed she'd never have another child. But one night she had a vivid dream of being surrounded by a circle of dancing children.

One little girl with brilliant amber eyes came forward and took her hand. 'I will be born again to you soon, mummy,' she said.

Very soon afterwards Anya unexpectedly found she was pregnant and gave birth to a beautiful daughter whose eyes became amber and grew up to look exactly like the girl in the dream.

If I had not experienced something similar myself I would perhaps have doubted the story which I heard from Anya's aunt some years later. I became unexpectedly pregnant with a third child as my first marriage was crumbling. The only person to be pleased was my young son who detected at once that I was pregnant and named the baby William.

I miscarried the baby at twelve weeks.

Some years later I remarried and had another son, Jack. But about six months after the birth, I started to see a little boy about three years old sitting at the foot of the stairs with blonde hair and blue eyes. He would disappear when my husband came home but we nicknamed my invisible child Eric.

I became pregnant again and Eric disappeared. Miranda was born and we joked we had our Eric after all. But a few months later Eric re-appeared though again only I could see him. At last we decided against the advice of everyone we did want another baby and true to form when I became pregnant Eric disappeared.

I gave birth to Bill, who at twelve months developed blonde hair and has retained his baby blue eyes.

Eric never appeared again — maybe it was getting a bit overcrowded even for him.

Of course one explanation of less exotic past life memories is that children are recalling some incident they sensed from the womb or in early childhood. Mary is now in her seventies but believes that she can remember before her birth. In the first version of this book I didn't include her story as it seemed so strange but in the intervening years I have learned that there is much that I don't understand and can only report. Mary wrote: 'My earliest memory is one briefly before I was born, simply being contained within my mother and a sense of weariness which I shared with her, her weariness and complete unawareness of me as a person.

'The second is of myself at about six weeks old. It was evening and I was completely outside myself looking down from a height and watching myself being bathed in an oval zinc bath beside an old-fashioned kitchen range. A woman was bathing me and a man sat on the other side of the fire. I did not know them. The woman said, "It's a shame and she's a such a lovely baby."

'I was vividly aware that I had come through a terrible experience and survived. I knew I had belonged closely to other people who were part of my awful agony. I knew I was now with strangers. It was a very vivid experience and must have happened in 1918. My father, I later found out, had been killed in France the day after I was born.

'My mother on hearing the news tried to commit suicide and so I was placed with foster parents.'

Ron who lives in Hertfordshire has what he believes is a very vivid pre-birth memory: 'As a very small child when I was hardly able to speak I had a terrifying recurring dream. I am now in my sixties but still have a vivid recollection of the terror. I was in the front ground-floor room of the house in which I then lived with my parents and was looking towards the bay window. Suddenly there was a high-pitched cry sounding like "yay-yay".

'My mother died from tuberculosis when I was four

years old. Many years later I was talking with my grand-mother and she remarked on my love of cats and said how strange it was since my mother had hated them. She told me that when my mother was pregnant with me she was sitting in the front room of our house when a cat jumped in through the bay window on to her lap.

'She was so terrified she almost miscarried. It seems to me that I was conscious and sharing the acute sensations experienced by my mother when I was in her womb.'

Children seem to have tantalising glimpses of the past but these are usually very fleeting. They are no less important to the child for that and should be valued and accepted whatever the source. Once we start testing them or questioning such experiences a child may feel pressurised to invent details or simply clam up.

Jilly Smith who lives in Lancashire told me: 'My husband Martin and I had just redecorated the study and bought a new lamp for the desk. It looked like an old-fashioned gas lamp and as soon as my son Adrian saw it he pointed and said, "Gas".

'He was just two and had a fairly basic limited vocabulary and hadn't even been with us when we bought it. Martin and I hadn't said anything and of course Adrian had never seen a gas lamp before.'

Jean's little daughter Bryony was three and not given to great flights of rhetoric. But at these apparent moments of past memory even the most reticent child may come out with quite complicated vocabulary and ideas of which afterwards he or she may have no recall. Bryony said suddenly: 'Mummy, why don't I have brown hair?'

Her mother explained that all the family had fair hair

200

and showed her family photos. But Bryony persisted and finally Jean ran out of patience and said, 'Because you haven't.'

'But I did have brown hair,' Bryony explained, 'before I was a baby when I used to look after the sick people in the Church.'

Bryony never mentioned the subject again. As I said these fleeting memories don't come complete with name, date and library references and if questioned the child clams up.

Adults too can suddenly recall a past childhood that seems to make sense of a present life. Sarah is now in her forties and involved in counselling the traumas of others. 'I always felt as a child alone and different. There was no-one in my family with whom I was in sympathy. I was a very withdrawn child, often retreating into silence for hours at a time. Although I think my family tried to show me love, I failed to respond to it.

'Then, years later, memories of another existence came flooding back. I saw myself on a ship, I knew I was going from England to another continent. I felt entirely alone and friendless. I knew I had been in an orphanage. I was about twelve.

'We reached Canada and I was sent to live on a farm. The farmer and his wife were not exactly cruel but conditions were harsh and I received no affection from them. Little things stick in my mind, hauling water from the well in the snow, the huge spiders in the wood-shed where I was sent to fetch logs. I was constantly cold and the thin clothes I'd been sent with didn't protect me. I died from pneumonia in my early teens. Strangely in my present life I was the only one of my family to suffer respiratory infections.

'A while after this memory came to me I heard a radio programme about Barnados children. At one time children from the Homes were sent to Canada and Australia to start a new life. For some of them it worked out well but others were extremely badly treated and because of this the practice was stopped.'

Lorna wrote: 'My daughter's baby was born on Christmas Eve. She was the first girl in the family. When she was six months old, she died. I kept saying, "She will come back". Two years later my daughter had another little girl with blue eyes just like the first.

'When Suzy was two years old, she accidentally found some photos of the baby's grave covered with flowers. She picked the photos up and ran to her mother and said "My flowers, mummy, mine, mine."

' "No," said her mother.

'But she kept insisting they were hers. "Dark, dark trees. Me frightened. Me go way. But me come back, Me not go away again."

'There was a row of tall trees near the baby's grave.'

Was Suzy the reincarnation of her dead sister? Or had she picked up conversations about her baby sister and perhaps half-understood they were taking flowers to her, so when she saw the photo with flowers decided to claim them.

Liz Cornish, a rebirthing expert based in London, believes that we choose the families we are born to because we have unfinished business that we need to resolve. Perhaps we have been in different relationships with them in the past. Why else, she says, do we generally chose such appalling parents!

This pre-natal selection could also be an attempt to find somewhere we might fit in. Buddhists believe a child is musical, not because of heredity or family influence, but because he or she was already musical and therefore chose to live in a musical family.

If this was ever proved to be true it would make the most wonderful counter-attack to the complaint that most parents hear at one time or another: 'I didn't choose to be born.'

How nice it would be if you were able to reply: 'Yes you did and not only that — you chose the wrong family as well. It's your fault and you're just going to have to make the best of it.'

Janet Boucher, the child psychiatrist, points out that there is no reason to assume that memory is something that is switched on the moment a child is born. He has already learned to recognise key voices even before birth. Even harder to explain is the fact that sometimes children seem to remember what appear to be snatches of past lives. But perhaps we have uncovered only the tip of the iceberg of human memory.

Adopted children will always wonder about their real parents and will often spend a great deal of time and effort in later life looking for them.

'I want to stay with you but I want to go back and see my other family,' is the type of plea that is familiar to many adoptive parents. But when this plea came from three-year-old James, it threw his mother completely.

He is her natural child and has never lived anywhere

else but their home. 'It all started gradually,' his mother Carolyn told me. 'James would talk about his other family but he was obviously anxious not to upset us. He said he had lived with another family before and he did want to be with us, but he would like to go and see them. At first we treated it very lightheartedly and humoured him.

'He talked about another father and mother and a sister, which was also strange because his own sister Sarah had not been born then. He also talked about a vehicle they used to have which appeared to be horse-drawn.

'There wasn't anything we could do because we didn't know where to take him to see this family, but it was awful because he was at one stage getting very distressed about not seeing them.'

It would have been a nice neat ending if James had been able to point to a white house and told the family: 'I used to live here.' But real life is all too often anything but neat. If the house existed his parents did not know where it was — or even if it was still standing after who knows how many years.

So Carolyn coped as best she could but not very successfully. 'He would say: "You know, when I lived in the white house", and became more and more distressed and started to cry, begging us to take him to the white house. "All right, I'll take you," I promised.

'But of course, I had no idea where it was and realised I had gone too far. There were tears on several occasions. "I want to go now, please take me," he used to say. It was so frustrating. We didn't know where to take him. "You know, you know," he would cry, Then it stopped.'

Was this a case of reincarnation or some sort of fantasy

world which took root in the boy's mind at a very early age? It raises many problems. Suppose James's parents had found a white house that fitted his description and there had been a family living there who had lost a son just before James was born.

What would their reaction have been if James had arrived and said: 'Hello I used to be your child.' It might have served only to reopen the wound of grief of the bereaved parents. They might have rejected James which would have been a severe psychological blow to the boy.

Or, worst of all, the bereaved parents might have demanded the return of 'their' child. A reincarnation custody case might not have stood up in court but the effect on James of having his loyalties suddenly split between past and present parents would have been horrific.

But even when there is no proof that memories of a past life are true, these memories can hold the key to problems now. We do not know whether they are actual memories or projection of present childhood or perhaps more likely the essence of other experiences concentrated and perhaps changed over time.

After all, we all tend either to sentimentalise or to dramatise our childhoods as we get older so if in your real past life you were a peasant in a straw hut you might be tempted to relocate the relevant experience to the castle up the road even if, like Sue ,you ended up in the dungeon.

Sue, for no apparent reason, was terrified of confined spaces and especially spiral staircases. During a session with a psychic counsellor she went back to a life which seemed to be set somewhere in the middle ages.

She felt herself reliving a childhood in which she was shut in a dungeon at the age of about 12 and left to die. 'There were rats and it was horrible,' she told me. Although she is now an adult and holds a responsible job Sue found herself so moved by the experience that she started to sob, 'I'm all alone and I'm going to die.'

The little boy that she was in her past life was taken down spiral stairs to the dungeon. As in conventional therapy, her psychic counsellor enabled Sue to relive the event then move away from it so that she could go forward. Freud's basic tenet is that all our traumas stem back to childhood. The question that Sue's experience raises is —which one?

Where past lives are concerned it is important to listen and take such memories seriously as even if we feel certain they are fantasy they are very real to the child and at the end of the day we really don't know.

But we can explain to a child that we can't go back to the past whether last year or last century and with a child's hazy sense of time scales a year may seem that long.

If children are given honest explanations they will accept that everything can't be resolved which is a good lesson in life. For creatures who inhabit the borders of fantasy and reality children can be remarkably realistic, more so than some adults who dream away their lives waiting for that golden tomorrow. Or pining for that golden yesterday which never existed outside their heads.

But perhaps there is yet another explanation of past lives certainly those that are triggered by a specific place? Are we picking up memories of past scenes that we apply to ourselves?

Ally and her family felt something at a 'new ancient monument'. Ally, who lives in North Carolina, wrote to tell me that while the family were travelling through British Columbia, in Canada, in the spring of 1989 they came across a hotel where the proprietor had put together a 'ghost' town from an collection of old buildings brought together from elsewhere.

'Included was a wonderfully restored saloon which we visited. The rest of the family had gone down the outside steps and was beginning to walk along the road when there was an agonised cry from Timothy, my four-year-old son, who was stumbling down the steps, clutching the back of his head and screaming that someone was trying to break his head.

'He described the pain as like a knife. I immediately thought of brain tumours, but neither before nor since has he ever complained of headache or pain. The situation we were in and the terror he exhibited for those few minutes convince me that he was, in fact, involved in an incident from the past.'

This might not be evidence enough to convince other people but as I have tried to show in this book the moments when our world brushes against the psychic world are fleeting: afterwards people can only say: 'Well this happened to me and it has changed my life in this way and I can find no other explanation for it.'

My own son, Jack ,also seemed to link into a past world when he was no more than four years old. For no apparent reason Jack came into our front room in Reading one afternoon and asked his dad if he knew anything about the old lady in the castle who'd been asleep in the sitting room.

Working out what he meant by the castle was no problem. The family had been to a huge old rectory in Theale, near Reading, Berkshire, that morning where a colleague of John's, the journalist David Addis, lived.

Jack had taken one look at the imposing stone building and said, 'Oh, a castle.' Then he'd gone off to play football in the garden and hadn't actually gone inside. But he obviously had a bee in his bonnet. 'You know, by the old church,' he said later over his tea.

David's house was, not surprisingly for a former rectory, next to the church.

'The old lady was in the chair in the sitting room,' Jack said. 'The guard was standing outside the door going in and out, in and out. He had a sword.'

'Like yours?' John asked. Jack had a fine collection of plastic swords and cutlasses.

'Not like mine. The guard's sword stood on the floor and went up and up and had one of those spades on the top. [This we worked out must be a halberd, the combination of a spear and an axe which Jack might have seen in some history book or on television.]

'The old lady died, you know. It was a Friday. The guard had opened the door because he heard a sound like a whistle and the smelly smoke came in and killed the old lady while she was asleep.

'When the smoke came out he closed the door and went upstairs.

'The guard didn't try to save the old lady because she was dying and he couldn't get the doctor because his doors were shut. It happened when it was dark.'

Jack was quite upset and John had to go off to to work

leaving me to cope as usual. Jack kept on to me, 'You know about the old lady' and I didn't seem able to give him the answer he needed, who she was and why she died. When Tom, Jack's eleven-year-old brother rang from Reading station to say he had returned from a trip and a friend's mum was dropping him home, Jack grabbed the phone and asked Tom if he knew about the old lady.

Over the next few days Jack kept mentioning her and the details were always the same and not at all embellished. But at last it died down.

Three months later out of the blue Jack started talking about the old lady again. We'd got through several plastic swords in the interim but he still insisted unprompted that the guard's sword wasn't like his but had a spade on top of a tall stick.

David who lives in the Rectory which only dates back to the eighteenth century didn't know if there had been an earlier building on the site — certainly the church is ancient. But I didn't bother to check. The old lady, whoever she was, was real to Jack. Was he slipping into a past life or picking up a picture from a past tragedy? Or has he a great future as a storyteller? Five years on Jack is fascinated by history.

Jane told me how her young son became distressed for no apparent reason: 'We were on holiday in the north of England and had gone to Warkworth Castle. As we were going round, Tom who was three or four became terrified to the point of distress and we had to take him out. At the time he was too frightened to talk but when he calmed down he told us he'd seen the head and shoulders of a man with an old-fashioned hairstyle and he remained distressed for some time and refused to go back into the castle.'

Transmigration between species is regarded as a distinct possibility by believers in reincarnation. A particularly noble creature may attain human rebirth while a worthless individual may be demoted.

But if we subscribe to the reincarnation theory then David, a perfectly ordinary schoolboy from Sibford school, had obviously lived a very worthy past existence.

He told me: 'I was playing crazy golf with a friend when an elderly lady approached me and said that she had seen me before. I had never seen her in my entire life but she insisted "Yes, I've definitely seen you somewhere before."

'By now we were thinking the old lady was senile. Then she said: "I know you. You were my pet dog who was killed by a garbage truck."

'Now we really were convinced that she was senile. "I can prove it," she said. "If you are my dog you should have a lump on the back of your neck."

'So to prove her wrong I felt behind my neck and there was the lump just where she said.'

Chapter Thirteen

Beyond The Body

THE TROUBLE WITH children is often that they do not know their limitations. In an episode from the Daily Mirror's Perishers cartoon strip Baby Grumpling is considering life and says to himself: 'If people can go forwards and backwards and sideways why can't they go up?' Seeing no good reason why they shouldn't, he starts to levitate. Then his sister, Maisie, arrives on the scene and tells him: 'Grumpling, if you want to live with people you've got to learn to obey the rules.'

Many children have broken bones to show for their early attempts at flying before they learned the rules. But some can remember breaking those rules and getting away with it.

Floating downstairs is very common in childhood but occasionally the results can be unpredictable. Jane described how when she was eight years old 'I floated upstairs and down again. The staircase turned at the top of the house and there was a bannister along the wall. It was a wonderful sensation and I floated back up again. I felt so powerful. Then I fell from top to bottom and never tried again. Mum didn't believe me at the time but now she understands.'

Mary recalled: 'It happened quite spontaneously when I was about three. I took off from the top of the stairs and floated below, alighting gently at the bottom.'

Clare says she often floated headfirst down the stairs in dreams as a child. 'Once though I actually found myself at the bottom of the stairs. I wasn't hurt, but I was really frightened. Nan and Grandad were in the sitting room with my mum and I can remember hiding behind my mum on the settee.'

Cicely says: 'I went to the staircase outside my bedroom door and took off, gliding gently down the stairs, head first I think. It was daylight, a summer evening. I think I was five years old, In those days one was sent to bed at set times, regardless of the light. The next night, I again went to the head of the stairs, but it did not work. I was extremely disappointed. Flying through the air was a wonderful sensation. If this was a dream, it was certainly no ordinary one.'

Lesley said she could remember floating downstairs as a child. 'When did it stop?' I asked her.

'When we moved into flats.'

Many children experience this floating down the stairs sensation. Though some of the heavier psychoanalysts can put 'deep' interpretations on floating and flying, from a psychological point of view it can perhaps be simply regarded as children testing the limits of their powers which of course they may greatly overestimate. Levitation has never been proven in a laboratory but there have been tests which have provided some evidence for the existence of 'out of body experiences', known as 'oobies'.

In these, the subject seems to leave his or her physical body behind and move around in a psychic body complete with arms and legs. I have heard of a number of cases in which 'oobies' happened quite spontaneously to children.

Lesley had her first out of the body experience when she was only seven. She told me: 'It was a sunny day I was sitting with my back against a bush. Suddenly I was in the red tree, sitting up there. I knew I was there. It was a copper beech tree and I could see myself sitting on the ground in the distance quite far away. I was very happy, hiding from people up there. There were lots of people around because there was a party at our house. Eventually. I got down from the tree and went back in my body.'

Lesley enjoyed her experience and it served as a means of escape from all the people whom she didn't want to mix with. 'It made me feel good,' she said. Lesley says she has had three 'oobies', one as a child, one as a teenager and one when she was twenty. Each time she thinks it was a specific sound that seemed to trigger off the experience. 'When I was very young, the first time, it was the sound of wheels. I think it was a pram going past,' she said.

Jean, a healer, told me her daughter used to play about when small by making her astral body run down steps in front of her physical body.

But an oobie can be terrifying if it occurs at night and the child feels totally out of control. Wanda writes: 'I was

213

five or six and we lived in a house with only one bedroom so when I was little I slept with my parents. I was feeling very ill and tired. I remember this floating feeling and as I drifted up to the window, I was actually standing next to it, only I was very small. I was standing on a kind of box with a rail of some sort. I remember looking down on myself and my parents. We were all asleep. I started to panic and shouted, "I want to go back". I kept saying that and calling my mother and crying at the same time. I couldn't understand why nobody heard me. Suddenly I felt a drifting and I was back in bed. I didn't go to sleep. I kept looking up to the wardrobe where I expected to go back any minute. I remember feeling so afraid. The experience was like there were two of you.'

Norma is in her seventies, but can still remember her frightening oobie at the age of eleven. 'I went to bed as usual, I was not ill or anything. That night I awoke but I had left my body and was looking down on myself sleeping from somewhere near the ceiling. It was an old house with high ceilings. From the ceiling protruded a hand, a right hand, a man's because there was part of a shirt cuff. I took hold of the hand and it began to draw me upwards and a voice I did not recognise as male or female said, "Come with me".

'I said, "No, I can't come", and let go of the hand. The next moment I was in my body again, gasping for breath and desperate to get enough air in my lungs. For a few seconds, I really thought I would die, but gradually I recovered. The picture today is as vivid as when it happened.'

Sylvia too believed for a moment that she was going to

die. 'It happened when I was eleven. I was lying in my bed and trying to get to sleep. Then I could see my own body lying on the bed and my sister who was in the bed next to mine. I didn't float to the ceiling but stayed suspended between the beds. But the strange thing was that I felt as if I was a mass of black dots. Next thing I knew I was back in my body and I told my mother I had thought I was dying. She gave me some brandy to calm me down.'

Were these bad dreams or did the children really leave their bodies? Many of the experiences happen at night or first thing in the morning. Is this because the conscious mind is at its least active, thus removing constraints on psychic activity?

Psychologists can argue that oobies result from the unfulfilled wishes projected on to a second life that the subject can control — a sort of super-self! This would be especially attractive to children. For quite young children, an out of the body type trance can be a way of escaping from a reality in which he or she may feel rejected.

Karl's need to feel powerful and superior to his companions with whom he was less able to compete in physical terms is implicated in his account of his out of the body experience as a teenager. 'I withdrew from the melee (of a football game with friends) and walked to the school gates. I started to feel sleepy — as if I was dropping into a trance. A soft breeze was blowing against my face. The evening was soft and warm. The warmth was more and more intense. I attempted to wake myself from this dream-like state, but found I could not. Suddenly I found myself above, way above, the others and my own physical body, calmly observing my friends. As I remained there, thirty feet above the ground, as if floating, I was in no way aware of being attached to a physical body or physical existence. It was as if part of my mind had decided to take its leave. I sensed a strange kind of dominance over my earthbound companions. I am up here. You are down there. At this, I felt even more satisfied, complete, above human understanding and knowledge.

'Suddenly one of my friends shouted my name. Yet the voice that replied so angrily, "Shut up", seemed more distant, yet was my voice, I am certain. My friend called out a second time. Suddenly, I leapt back into my body. Then I remained rooted to the spot, dazed and confused.'

Karl says he was unfit. Perhaps this made him feel inferior to his friends who at that age tend to scorn a weakness at sport in boys. It is just as difficult for a teenager who wants to be an individual to rebel against the culture of other teenagers as it is to rebel against parents. How wonderful to prove you are different and a cut above the rest by flying.

But Flo's oobie stopped her from getting the attention she so desperately wanted. 'I am 65,' she wrote. 'When I was 12 I was in bed with a nervous breakdown for weeks. I had a strange childhood. My father did not live with us and I never remember sitting down at the same table with him even for a cup of tea. Money was tight and sometimes we could not even afford food. In my illness, I wouldn't eat, no couldn't eat, and I was skin and bone. I lay in the upstairs front bedroom of the house for hours on end and nobody came near me except my mum and she was so busy she did not come very often.

'We couldn't really afford a doctor (in those days you

had to pay for a visit) but I was so ill that for the first time in my life mum said the doctor would come to see me. I was thrilled to have someone to talk to apart from my mum. I heard the doctor come upstairs and pause on the landing. The door opened and in he came but he didn't talk to me at all. He was looking at somebody in the bed and I was up on the ceiling above the mantelpiece. I spoke to him but he ignored me and I was disappointed and then angry and thought: "Well who is he looking at down there?" and that split second I found that I had moved over the room with no conscious effort and was looking over the doctor's shoulder and then to my amazement I saw myself. I do not remember any more.

'I seemed to know instinctively not to tell anyone else or they would laugh. Those feelings are as clear today as if they happened only yesterday.'

Youngsters who experiment with oobies can some-times go a bit too far. Alan explains: 'When I was ten, I was given permission to stay up late to listen to the radio. The time was about 9.30pm. I remember clearly thinking it must be possible for your spirit/soul to detach itself from the physical body and roam free. I sat still. I don't know for how long when I realised all was still and silent and I was truly free. I was not frightened and decided to look at myself. This I did and in fact was studying myself hard when suddenly I was conscious of a movement on my left hand side and the kitchen door opened. My sister Eleanor walked in. She looked at my physical body and screamed. Without any effort on my part, I found myself whole again.

'I asked my sister if she was all right. She was very

upset and told me she thought I was dead. She said I was totally empty like a shell. I was going to tell her when she became pretty angry and accused me of trying to frighten her. She threatened to tell my parents but I reached a pact with her, though I did not tell her what had really happened.'

Gordon frightened himself with his oobie when he was 14. For a year he had been experimenting with his dreams, trying to control them. 'My mother used to call me every morning in time for breakfast and work (I started on my fourteenth birthday at the local docks). One trick I played on her was to rattle my shoes under my bed and shout "I'm coming". This particular morning, I must have dropped back into a doze. My mother lost her temper. She came upstairs and gave a sharp knock on my door. "Gordon, get out of bed."

'Immediately, I found myself suspended above my body and bed, about one foot in distance. I clearly saw my body on the bed below. The situation was very real, indeed more real than most of life's experiences. "God, I'm dead," I thought. I embraced my body below on the bed, thinking, "I've got to get back". I hugged the body with my arms. I remember looking up at the ceiling with relief. I was back in my body again. At the same time, I could feel my heart pounding fast and I remember my mother entering the room and remarking "What on earth's wrong with you?"

' "Oh, I'll be all right in a minute or two," I said. "Go away. I'll be down soon."

'With hindsight, the remarkable thing was she did just that. The effect of my experience was an overwhelming sense of security. Life does not stop here on earth. The only problem has been getting anyone to believe me.'

Psychic forms may not have been detected under laboratory conditions but according to accounts I have come across close relatives sometimes perceive them. When Connie was a teenager, she was very ill in hospital with meningitis. 'After my parents had visited me, they went home and went to bed. My mother said to my father that I was in bed with them. Then my father could also feel my presence. The following evening when they visited me, I told them I had slept with them that night. From that day I started to recover.'

Though Connie's parents did not actually see her, they felt her presence. Had both parents and child tuned in at a time of distress when each would be thinking of the other? Bedtime when a child is absent is particularly poignant and Connie was probably thinking of home and family? Or did Connie 'travel' home for comfort? The experience or her belief in it may have triggered some psychological strength in Connie that gave her immune system a kick.

Pauline often visited her father, Phil, who had separated from her mother, and got on very well with his new partner, Mandy. He had tried to reassure the little girl that although he didn't live with her all the time 'I'll always be there if you need me'. Kids are notorious for taking parents at their word, often with bizarre results. Phil and Mandy were sitting watching television, when Phil felt a chill run through him and all the hairs on the back of his neck standing on end. But men can be very unobservant. It was Mandy who eventually said: 'Can't you see her sitting over there — it's Pauline?' His little girl had apparently 'popped back' in her astral body to test dad's words!

Oobies seem to be related to a phenomenon described as the 'near death experience' or NDE which is reported by people who have come close to death through illness or accident. They seem to leave their bodies and glimpse some sort of afterlife.

David Lorimer, director of the International Association for Near Death Studies, has received many accounts from adults and teenagers relating childhood as well as more recent NDEs. Children's reports of NDEs differ from those of adults in that, although they are less elaborate they have a special pictorial quality.

Phoebe had a very bad attack of scarlet fever when she was 17 before the second world war. She was not expected to last the night in the old fever hospital where she was cared for by nuns. Later in life, she told her daughter that she remembered looking down on her body that was lying on the bed and the nuns and the doctor standing next to it. She remembers feeling very much at peace and floating down a spiral. She could hear soothing music, but it was not being played on any specific instrument. She was going down the spiral into something clean, white and cotton-woolly.

Suddenly Phoebe felt something cold pressed on her forehead and was back on the bed. A nun had put a cold sponge on her head. Without this intervention, Phoebe would have gone on down the spiral as she saw a shadow beckoning her. It did not have a face, but was a nice shape.

Her daughter, Jan, did not know about her mother's experience until she was 15 and angry that her grandfather had died. Jan asked her mother what the point of living was if it always ended in death. Phoebe told her the story and said that since then she had not been afraid of dying.

Very young children have reported NDEs. Pauline was not much more than two when 'I was given up by the doctors when I almost died of pneumonia. I seemed to pass through a dark tunnel, not very pleasant, then skipped along on bright green grass holding someone's hand. I did not know who it was, only that I was very, very happy and I think it was a man. I remember the hand and half the arm but what sticks in my mind is the green grass.'

The simplest stories involve the child floating above his or her body. Mike was nearly five. 'It was Christmas. I remember it as if it was yesterday. I was very excited that Christmas was almost upon us in spite of the war. I remember rushing out to buy my dad cigarettes in the freezing weather without a coat before my mother could stop me. Anyway the next thing I recall I was extremely ill, so much so that my mother set up a bed for me in the front room next to the fire. After that I don't remember much except for one vivid memory. Suddenly I was in a position near the door, looking across at the corner where my bed was.

'Everything, including my mind was crystal clear. I could see myself lying on the bed, blond-haired and angel-faced, with my eyes closed. I remember being fascinated at the sight of my nostrils pumping in and out as I laboured to breathe and I remember thinking, "Wow, I do look sick".

'Being over the door at this point and being so young, I assumed that everybody could see themselves without

221

having to be in their bodies. This was my last thought before I was aware of a cold stethoscope being pressed to my chest and seeing my old family doctor looking at me and saying to my mother, "You almost lost him. He's got pneumonia and only pulled through with your care." '

Oona also had very bad pneumonia when she was about seven. 'I can recall being in my parents' bed in my parents' bedroom with a fire in the grate. I was very hot, in pain and distressed. The next second I was high above, looking down and all the pain was gone. I floated above the bed and looked at myself and my parents and felt a bit sad for them, but happy for myself that I could leave my body behind. As I turned to the top corner of the room, out of the golden haze, my mother's voice said, "Oona, oh, Oona," and the next minute I was back in my bed with all the pain.

'Afterwards I looked back on the experience with some surprise, but dared not relate it to anyone for fear of ridicule. But it was so real to me and still is that I have never feared death since. If this life was all we had, then it would be illogical and rather a poor deal for some.'

Marie's experience as a child of three or four was also very simple. 'There was a flooded mine close to our house and while I was playing, I slipped and was washed away. I scrabbled frantically and was rescued by workmen nearby. I put up a plucky fight but unfortunately got some water in my lungs. I became very ill and was at death's door. I remember clearly in the middle of the night my father looking down on me and I said, "I have just been flying very fast through a tunnel with a light at the end". He told me I had been seeing my own bedside light which was a small paraffin lamp (we had no electricity). I loved

222

my dad and accepted his explanation and never spoke of it again.'

The childhood memories of NDEs retain their grip through life. One lady of eighty recalled: 'When I was seven, I had measles and was very ill. How long I lay there I don't know but I was in a lane where there were very high ornamental gold gates. Inside was the most beautiful garden, no lawn, path or anything, but flowers of every kind. Those that attracted me most were the Madonna lilies, delphiniums and roses, but there were many, many more. I thought how I would love to go in.

'I pushed the gates and they gave way, but try as I might I could not get in. There was something behind me or on both sides that seemed to be stopping me. I was so upset but in the end I gave up trying. I opened my eyes and saw my mother and father crying. My mother looked at me and almost shouted, "Look, dad". I never told anyone, but I can remember it as if it was yesterday.

Rob saw his mother trying to pull him back. He was nine and a first appendix operation had left part of the organ still inside him and it burst. 'By the time of my second operation, my condition was serious and at one point clinical death occurred. I can only recall two images: the first was looking down on my body on the operating table and being turned over by green-clad surgeons and nurses. This image is particularly vivid and despite its goriness was not associated with any pain or distress.

'The second image is of a blackness with a pinpoint of light far off in the distance. I felt drawn to the light, but there was a feeling that I did not want to pull towards it. My mother is with me in this scene trying to pull me back from the light. There is also a wind rushing past towards the light. Again this image is startlingly clear, unlike many other things I remember from that time. I remember little else except coming round after the operation in total panic, made worse by the fact that I couldn't move due to the after-effects of the anaesthetic I assume.'

For some people, the childhood NDE is not only more real than reality, but colours their whole attitude to life. They may feel that they should have died and even in extreme cases attempt suicide.

Josie had her NDE while suffering from peritonitis and says: 'I seemed to float along an empty corridor towards and then into a brilliant light with indefinable shades of pastel-like colours. There were what I can only describe as billions of beautiful shimmering forms, no outlines as they were all cloaked in whitish-like garments of translucent light. I longed to be able to tell my parents not to grieve. If only they knew how joyously happy I was, they would rejoice instead.

'I often wish I had not been brought back and then I would not have had to live through the many problems that have beset my life and I would have died in total peace. Death can come at any time and I have no fear of it.'

Josephine is now 22 but her life since her NDE during an operation in France as a child of 12 has been spent trying to recreate her experience. 'Everything went too fast for me,' she recalls. 'One minute I was in a deep dark sleep and then suddenly I was in a place with mid-pinkish clouds everywhere, hazy, soft, pinkish, light, very comforting. Next I was wandering through rooms. There was beautiful music. It was so smooth, soft and harmonious. I was so much at ease and felt so relieved and peaceful. I floated through these rooms at a higher level than I walked at that age. In fact it seemed, I nearly grazed the ceiling. It seemed to me we were looking for something. Some quiet presence was with me.

'Then we were in a room and there below me the doctors, masked and gowned, bent over what was me. "More glucose," one was saying. Then I had a shock. It seemed like they were talking right next to me, yet I was looking at them from above. "Which do you wish?" insisted the presence. "You don't have to go back. The choice is up to you." There was no pressure to choose but I thought about mum and dad. In a flash, I was back in the operating theatre. A voice said firmly. "She is waking".

'I must have been given some more anaesthetic because all I can remember is grasping someone's hand hard and drifting back into normal sleep. For me no whoosh or warning I was about to return. It was a great shock that happened at the moment I thought about my loved ones. The experience made me feel very strange. I spoke to no-one about it. I became either very enthusiastic about things or depressed as I remembered how happy I had been in that state. I am now 22 and at last have learned to control my desire to return.

'I once worked at a fun fair when we lived in the United States, taking rides in a desperate attempt to create the feeling of flying. I cut my hair and had it dyed red and took delight in anything pink and puffy. While I lived with my parents, I could control my desire to return, but the moment I came back to England to university, it was all set free.

225

'Sometimes I seemed to be controlled by something that was not me and I wondered if I had brought something back with me. I have so regretted this choice I had but did not take, though there are times I am proud of my choice.'

There is so much controversy over whether such experiences are scientifically verifiable that the people who have them sometimes get forgotten by science and they are left to struggle alone with the burden of their experience.

While some NDEs leave a scar, others are quite magical. With young children religion and magic can be mixed together; especially as nativity plays at school with the tinselly angels are often followed closely by a party where Father Christmas and his elves turn up. Perhaps that is why in hospital at Christmas, Megan, then aged 10, saw not an angel, but Father Christmas.

'I had a big operation on my shoulder for a useless arm damaged at birth. My mother had died giving birth to me. I was told later I nearly died during the operation. I had the last rites of the church which I do not remember. I had been looking forward to Christmas even though I was in hospital. What I saw was the most lovely bright light. Then I saw Father Christmas going through that lovely ray of light. I could see him going up and up. Before he got to the top, I heard someone call my name, "Meg, Meg," which they used to call me in those days. The bright light seemed to fade away from me. Father Christmas was gone when I felt someone holding my hand, saying, "Don't die, Meggie". I opened my eyes to see my father crying and then I began to recover. I will never forget that wonderful light, a light I have never seen again.'

The vividness and strange imagery of six-year-old Jacques' NDE were not those of a child's normal visions of angels or God. 'When a youth, I had a fall of some considerable height, landing head first on concrete. When I arrived at the hospital the doctors pronounced me dead and issued a death certificate. My parents were told I must be interred at once — we were living in the tropics at that time. They would not agree and I was placed in a room that was in the main constructed of marble and left there three days.

'On the third day, a nurse came in and saw a slight movement and found that I was alive.

'All I can recall is that I was walking along a rough-hewn tunnel with walls that looked as if the rocks were of copper and gold lit by firebrands on the walls. I felt no fear and continued down the tunnel till I came to a round chamber cut in this strange rock of copper and gold and there seated on a marble seat of very beautiful design was this enormous figure of a man in a white robe with long, flowing white hair and beard. He looked as old as time itself and yet as young as a boy. I made as if to run towards this force of love, strength, power, light and perfection. Suddenly, a look of foreboding came on his face. He raised his hand and I could go no further. Then with a lovely smile, that hand gently pushed me back with the words, "Not now, not now," echoing in my ears. It was then I shall always believe I came back from the dead.'

Frances said: 'In 1914 or 1915 when I was four or five years old I was very ill. At the same time my father was very ill in another room with double pneumonia and pleurisy.

227

'There was a nurse looking after us both and my mother was dividing her time between my father and me. At that time I was an only child.

'Quite suddenly I became aware of a shiny white person (my description afterwards to my mother) standing at the foot of my bed. I still remember this quite clearly. He was radiating light and he had no wings.

'He asked if I would like to go away with him and I saw a lovely place with green grass and sunshine and children playing. It was clear to me that I had a choice and I felt a longing to go. But then I thought that my mother would not be able to manage without me and so refused.'

Chapter Fourteen

The Final Mystery

NICHOLAS WAS ONLY seven when he was admitted to the ward where Jane was nursing. He was suffering from cystic fibrosis and the long-term prospect was not good at that time, almost 20 years ago. Jane said: 'He was very poorly and not responding to drugs and treatment. He deteriorated during the later part of the night and it looked as if he would not turn the corner. He was being cared for mainly by his parents and the nurses were in and out of the single room he had been given, checking everything was all right, but trying not to be intrusive. He was being cuddled on his mother's lap, when he opened his eyes and said: "Mummy, I can see the angels". Soon afterwards he died.'

Another girl was described by her mother as having a look of 'pure wonderment' at the moment of death.

Physiological theories have been advanced about what

happens in our bodies and brains to cause such deathbed visions. But it is perhaps a fallacy that a physiological explanation must be 'the correct one' and of course no one has reliably been able to quantify death itself. Tessa Williamson, a bereavement counsellor at the Helen House Hospice for terminally ill children in Oxford, has noticed that dying children do seem to mature very suddenly and it may be that at death they are able to share with their parents and nurses the glimpse they catch of another world as they leave this one.

Monica who lives in South London told me the story of Brigid, a little girl who was desperately ill with leukaemia. On the night she died her father went into her room and Brigid said excitedly, 'Hello, daddy, there's going to be such a rumpus in the morning. The real Brigid's coming back. I'm not the real Brigid you know.'

Debbie had a vision of her own death two years before it happened. Her mother, Dionne, recalled: 'One morning when my daughter was ten she felt very poorly. I tucked her up in bed and went downstairs to make her a cup of tea. While the kettle was boiling, I popped back to check on her. Debbie was lying on the bed with her eyes open and she was very still. I called her name but she didn't move. I panicked and put my arms around her and started gently to shake her calling her name all the time. Suddenly she blinked and was back with me.

'Debbie told me she was floating down a long tunnel and at the end of the tunnel there was a shining bright light. But before she reached the light I'd woken her up. Unbeknown to us Debbie had started a long battle against liver cancer. My beloved daughter died two years later. We discussed the afterlife a lot. I wanted her to know there was something better to go when we die and towards the end of her life several things happened to convince us life does go on.'

Children are sometimes seen at the moment of death surrounded by a halo of light by people who care for them as well as close family. They may appear suddenly in the night and the next morning the news of their death comes. But when Michael died, his therapist, Carole, saw his older brother ringed in light. Carole who lives in Reading described: 'I was working as a play therapist and became very fond of Kim, a nine-year-old boy whose brother Michael was suffering from cancer in his right eye. Michael was only four and I got to know him too as he'd come along to the group when he was well enough. He was a very brave, cheerful chap and everyone was optimistic he'd pull through. One night Kim appeared to me surrounded in a beautiful white light and told me his brother had died.

'The next day I went to work and the news came during the morning that Michael had died suddenly at the time I had seen Kim.

'I didn't tell anyone but when I was talking to his mother after the funeral she told me that she'd known Michael was going to die because two or three days before his death he had suddenly told her, "I can see millions of flowers. Mummy, will you come with me?" '

For a child, when a parent dies, his world is turned upside down. He feels angry and betrayed that his parent has left him. Prue remembers losing her father when she was in her late teens. 'One day, soon after his death, I was

231

feeling so utterly weary and wondering if it really was worth living, battling on without support and guidance that for a fleeting moment I was tempted to think what was the use of living. Momentary though this was, I knew my father was standing by the window. He was deeply concerned about me and I heard him say, "You cannot reach me that way".

'Then he was gone, but the feeling persisted that he was still deeply concerned about me. The realisation that he was still caring about me and my future life grew stronger and I plodded on and gradually over the years never had any more doubts about life after death or of trying to hasten my own end.'

Janet Boucher, the child psychiatrist, says that when a child sees a ghost, he is in a sense saying the person has not died. She feels that initially, seeing the ghost need not be harmful and can be good. 'What is worrying from the psychiatric point of view is that by keeping the ghost the person will never resolve the grief reaction.'

But in this case, seeing her father helped a grieving and suicidal girl to overcome her despair and what she kept was the feeling that he did still care about her life.

Even a young child will try to make sense of death, whether of a beloved relative or even a much loved pet. He has to explain it to himself in his own terms. Ally from North Carolina, USA, told me of her son William who lost his pet cat in an accident when he was two-and-a-half. 'William sat quietly curled up in a chair for a while and then came out with, "I guess it's just the fur that dies".'

Alice came from a farming family. When she was 11 she was sent to boarding school and missed her mother desperately, as they had been very close. 'When I was 12, I went home and found my mother terribly thin and frail. I implored her to see a doctor, but she refused to go while I was home. She cried when I left for school which was unusual and three days later she died. Her body lay in the guest room at home and when no one was around, I crept in to look at her.

'I drew back the sheet and instead of looking at peace, she looked as if she had screamed at the end and her lips were curled back over her teeth. She had been in pain to the last and I have never forgotten that. I couldn't cry and I couldn't eat or sleep.

'I dreamt one night I stood outside a door. I was very upset and hammered on the door. It opened slightly and I jammed my foot in to keep it open. I saw my mother in a room full of light. She seemed to be greeting old friends. Suddenly, she turned, put a finger up and came towards me. She said: "I'm happy here. Please go away. You cannot come here yet." The door closed. I started to become well, for I believed she was happy at last.'

For a sibling to disappear and for the parents to be distraught with grief for the lost child can be utterly confusing for the children left behind. When he was seven, the author J.M. Barrie lost his elder brother David in a skating accident. From being the carefree youngest brother, he found himself faced by the impossible task of trying to take the place of his mother's favourite child. He became driven by the desire to imitate David so well that his beloved mother would not notice the difference. Wearing his dead brother's clothes, he burst into his mother's room and began whistling in the special way that David used to do. It was not until many years later that he realised how deeply he must have hurt his mother.

I discussed this with Tessa Williamson who said it is devastating for the child left alive to feel that the parent wants the dead child, not him. 'The message is loud and clear. She wants my dead brother, so if I try to be him, then maybe she'll want me.' This was not the case and Barrie never got over this, nor the feeling he had to make it up to his mother by taking his brother's place.

Janet Boucher feels that this glorification of the dead child can be permanently damaging to the surviving child's esteem. One eighteen year old she knew, whose twin had died in childhood was still haunted by the feeling that the wrong twin had died. As she points out, the worst aspect is that children believe that only old people die. So when a young person dies, it threatens the whole fabric of their world. They fear that they too may die.

For Joanna, her sister, Sylvia, who died at the age of six was blonde and angelic and a good child, although Joanna said, she must have been naughty sometimes. 'People used to say Sylvia was too good for this life,' said Joanna and she remembers as a child thinking: 'If I died, they'd think I was perfect,' and being desperately unhappy. Now middle-aged she has always felt she had to live up to the memory of her dead sister.

Joanna's mother, Sally, was never aware that her surviving daughter felt second best but Sylvia's death still haunted her many years later. Like many mothers who have lost young children, Sally believes that Sylvia is still with her: 'The Christmas before Sylvia died we decided to have a New Year party for the children and so my husband

Bill said, "Leave the decorations up for a few more days. It won't hurt."

'I was worried because of the old superstition that it was unlucky to keep Christmas decorations up after January 6. When a child dies you look for reasons and signs and I suppose I'll always feel guilty that I didn't take the trimmings down.

'On the night my little girl died it was terribly windy and all night there was a yellow light moving all around the room. Early in the morning the police arrived to tell me that Sylvia had gone so suddenly it hadn't been possible to fetch us.

' "It was that light," I said to Bill.

' "Did you see it too?" Bill asked. "Why didn't you say something? I thought I was going mad." '

Not only lights can herald death of child. In the mid 1930s Margaret was living in the wilds of County Clare in Ireland with her husband and three month old baby. In the middle of the night the couple woke up and could hear solemn music outside the window. It sounded as though a band was playing at a Wake but there was no other house for miles and no lights broke the darkness. So they checked the baby and went back to sleep. When they woke in the morning the baby, a perfect, healthy child had died in the crib.

The death of a grandparent, though obviously sad for the child who may lose someone very special in his life, is more in the natural order of things.

When Geraldine's grandad died, she was able to share the time leading up to his death. This helped her to cope even as a child with not only the loss of a beloved grandparent, but with the questions thrown up by death. 'I loved my grandfather dearly. When I was a child, he used to play his concertina for me and sang me many little songs. Then he became very ill. He had cancer and my mother nursed him at our house. One night I was sitting at his bedside and he looked up and smiled at someone I couldn't see. He said, "You've come for me," and the room was filled with an unearthly kind of love and peace and my grandfather looked so calm and happy, instead of the suffering of his pain. The next morning he was dead. I looked at his dead body and knew I wasn't looking at my grandfather. His soul was my real grandfather.'

This would have been a nice chapter ending but I was aware that I was evading a painful issue. To write merely of paranormal incidents concerning children and death seemed to be dodging the issue so I went to Helen House Hospice for terminally ill children to talk to Tessa Williamson and to see how bereaved families coped.

Though I very much wanted to visit the hospice, like all parents I was scared of facing the prospect of children who were no different from my own except that they were condemned by disease to an early and inevitable death.

I need not have been scared of Helen House for while it is a place where children come to die at the same time it is a hopeful, happy place where many children spend days of pleasant life. Much of the work is in giving support to families involved in a long-life threatening illness that may last for months or even years.

I glimpsed one or two children. One I was told was very sick indeed. Another was obviously quite badly handicapped. The children who die there can die with their families around them with the minimum of pain in lovely surroundings where they and their family will be supported and encouraged and cared for.

Afterwards the body will be placed in a little bedroom where the parents and other children can see the dead child, touch the body and ask questions, so there is no terror for the children left of a brother or sister going into hospital and apparently just disappearing. This is the process that Tessa Williamson refers to as 'making death real'.

A very small child had died not long before I arrived. A little cot for the dead child was made up in the little bedroom and there was a child's puzzle in the corner.

Living and dying are very homely affairs at Helen House. No one wears a uniform and everyone shares the chores in the modern building with huge windows, set round an enchanting garden. There was a tape of children's songs playing, colourful wall-hangings, soft settees and carpets and an Aladdin's cave of a toy cupboard for the brothers and sisters as well as the sick child. The only reminder this was not some sort of luxury hotel for children was the box labelled 'Toys for blind children' in the cupboard.

There was a room where the children could do messy activities and even a whirlpool bath, used by patients, staff, mums, dads and brothers and sisters alike — 'great fun for children who couldn't move much', said Tessa. Mums and dads can stay at Helen House along with brothers and sisters, occasionally grandparents and even the odd pet.

The eight children's bedrooms are free of the usual

hospital smell or hospital machinery — deliberately, because the children have had enough of that.

'Many parents do report a sense of a presence after the child's death — being aware that he is with them, not actually seeing him, but feeling that he is around,' said Tessa. 'They say after a year or so that the presence is gone. It usually is a good feeling that the child is still there. One mum was certain that the child's toys had been moved around.

'In my experience bereaved parents on the whole find spiritualism unhelpful. They may need to find an answer and sometimes feel the need to experiment. But what they want is to have the child back and to be told he is trying to get in touch rubs it in even more. They are still divided even if there is contact.'

I remembered a story told to me of Sarah, who lost her two-year-old in an accident. She had a recurring dream that she was allowed to take the child out of his grave for an hour every day. She took his pushchair down to the grave to collect him, but did not want to take him back.

Her desire to have her son return to her is echoed through the ages by countless mothers. Their lament has passed into folklore and songs such as the Wife of Usher's Well which relates how the mother of three sons who were lost at sea cried out:

I wish the wind may never cease
Nor fishes in the flood
Till my three sons come home to me
In earthly flesh and blood.

Her wish is granted and the sons return for the night but as soon as the cock crows they have to return to the gates of paradise. There can be no permanent reunion for mother and son in this world.

'The whole point of grieving is to accept and recognise that death is final,' said Tessa. 'Searching is part of eventually accepting that the child is not going to return to his body. Coming to terms with it is a huge thing.

'The second year is worse than the first. By the second year, parents can no longer pretend the child has just gone on a long holiday. If someone has lost her only child or all of the children through a hereditary illness, to the casual question "Do you have children?', either answer can cause anguish.

'If you say no then not only are you betraying the child by implying that it never lived but also you may be suggesting that you are against children in some way and all the prejudices and tactless remarks can be trotted out.

'To say, "I had a child but he died" can cause problems for other people especially if they are comparative strangers. Families with several children with a hereditary illness can go from two or more children to none.

'The loss of a child is perceived by people in general as an outrage. It is seen as wrong, against the pattern of life of growing up and the hope that the child will have children of his own some day. It is hard for the family and hard for people who come across them. A person can be a child at any age, If someone dies at 60 before his parents who are still alive at 80, it is still perceived as wrong.

'Death is not seen as part of life and people are not comfortable around the idea. Death is guaranteed to happen to all of us. But when it happens to a child, it is out of key and even more of a no-go area. Parents are trying to make sense of their loss. Families who have lost a child say that things in life that were important before, such as buying a new car and status things have become completely irrelevant. It can change their attitude to life. Often a father will pack in a highly paid job, because he has realised that money cannot buy a child's life.

'Quite a few mothers threaten to commit suicide to try to be with their dead children. But I try to tell them that we have no idea what happens after death and that they may not be with their child. There is terrific stress in having a child ill over a period of time, months, even years and it can be a great strain especially on the mother coping with the everyday care.

'The child may be the only thing that is keeping the parents together. When the child does die, the parents may be far apart. Mum has cared for the child twenty four hours of the day and night. Dad may have to keep on his job. Both will be exhausted. The relationship ceases to be a growing thing. Everything is channelled into the sick child. When the child dies they are complete strangers. Some families split up before the child dies.

'The brothers and sisters are encouraged to be involved in the dying and share it. If the families want it, they can be there at the moment of death. Quite a number spend time with the body afterwards. The siblings are encouraged to be involved to let death be real to them. The sisters and brothers may ask: "How do I know my sister is dead?" It is important that the dead child should not just disappear.

'It is important for the child to feel that the body is cold. They are shown how to feel the dead child's pulse and this is compared with their own pulse to demonstrate the difference. They may hold a mirror up to their mouth and then to the dead child's so they can see with their own a mist forms on the mirror. Death is allowed to become real for them. They observe the change in a dead child's appearance even after a short time. It is amazing how the dead child seems suddenly to age. The family come to realise the body is only an empty shell. They find it very comforting that what was vital has gone.'

Tessa often uses the analogy of the chrysalis and the butterfly. The beautiful part, the butterfly part, she says has flown away. The idea is not new. The butterfly was an ancient Greek symbol for reincarnation and St Theresa of Avila in the mid-sixteenth century used the idea of the caterpillar emerging from the cocoon as a symbol of resurrection.

But it was not until the pioneering work of Elizabeth Kubler-Ross into death and children dying that these ideas were applied to help children and adults to come to terms with death.

Tessa might tell the brothers and sisters to think of a tent. The tent is our body. When the tent gets ragged and torn, you have to abandon it.

The child who is left may need a lot of reassurance since he or she may have fought with the dead brother or sister at some time, as all children do, and shouted: 'I wish you were dead.' Suddenly the child is dead and the one left alive needs to know that those words did not kill. Remember Freud's fear as a child, that his jealousy had killed his 15-month-old brother Julius.

'The death of a child is not something that will go away

quickly. Parents will get over it but only in their own time. One mother after three-and-a-half years waking up with a stabbing pain said she still felt a sadness but it had become copeable with. She said she did not want the sadness to go away,' said Tessa.

'Another said on the tenth anniversary of her first child's cot death though she had four more children, with tears in her eyes. "A little bit will always be sad."

'Parents always need the little bit of sadness there for the child existed and does not exist any longer.'

Chapter Fifteen

Are All Kids Psychic?

Y OUNG CHILDREN DON'T make any big deal out of a psychic experience. Indeed they may be totally amazed that mum can't see the old man sitting beside her on the settee. As for disappearing into thin air — why, people do it all the time on the television and young children rarely worry about logistics.

After Sharon's marriage broke up she went back home to live with her mum in Reading taking her two-and-a-half-year-old son Richard and his 18 month old sister. Sharon explained: 'I was sitting on the floor in the lounge holding the little one and Richard was playing with his toys. The room was an extension to a much older house. Suddenly Richard pointed to the other end of the room and said quite casually, "Look, mummy, there's a man."

' "Oh yes," I said thinking he was playing a game. But Richard continued to watch and became quite cross. "Do move your legs, mummy so the man can get past." Then he went on playing and never mentioned the man again. I was quite scared when I realised he wasn't pretending because my younger brother had some years before seen a man walk into his room in front of my dad and promptly disappear. Dad had seen nothing.'

For many children, psychic experiences fade as they get older to emerge only in crisis. And support from a sympathetic parent is vital for as the child grows older it can be a burden to know things we cannot change — though if we do listen to children then we can perhaps save ourselves coming a cropper.

It is important that our children can talk to us about their fears, however seemingly irrational they are, and be reassured that they aren't responsible for events they may predict.

Teresa felt responsible for years for a crash she foretold though no one was hurt. When Teresa was eight she was looking forward to going out in her aunt's car as usual on Saturday afternoon. It was always a treat as they stopped somewhere nice for tea on the way back. But suddenly Teresa had the most dreadful feeling that the car would crash and told her mum. Her mother was cross and told her she was being silly and if she mentioned anything to Aunty she'd get a smack.

Teresa couldn't forget her premonition. All the time they were out Teresa was terrified but didn't dare say a word. When they finally pulled into Teresa's street she heaved a sigh of relief but at that moment a van pulled out of the side road and went into the side of Aunty's car. Teresa's mum insisted it was pure coincidence and Teresa never told anyone about the incident till she was a mother herself.

If the child is distressed by a ghost or invisible friend turned malevolent it is vital to see the problem through the child's eyes and help him or her to overcome the problem. Above all we need to out right any earthly traumas in the child's life.

Jodie was seven when things started flying out of her wardrobe and hitting her. She was convinced there was a demon with black eyes who came out at night and she refused to go to bed. Mum was at the end of her tether. She'd remarried a year before and had a new baby to cope with. But it wasn't enough to explain Jodie's poltergeist away as attention seeking because it was terrifying the child.

Fortunately Jodie's mum didn't tell her she was being silly and moved Jodie's bed in with the baby. She spent time in the old bedroom with Jodie during the day and even took the door off the wardrobe as it was carved and quite scary. Jodie helped to rearrange the furniture and choose new curtains. Finally Jodie moved back in, keeping a night light burning and a 'magic bell' to call Mum if she was afraid. Mum made sure Jodie had plenty of attention when the baby was asleep and the poltergeist disappeared. Jealousy of the baby or jealous feelings that triggered off a psychic attack matters less than that the problem was resolved.

But childhood psychic experiences can be positive if sensitively handled and actually help a nervous child to feel special and overcome earthly fears. Rhona explained how her angel stopped her fearing the dark: 'When I was

12 I saw an angel. I remember waking one night and looking at the top of my bed there it was, about two feet high. It had a long white garment with a yoke and a halo around its head. The hands were joined as though in prayer. Somehow I knew I must not speak to it or it would go away. So I went back to sleep. I was not so afraid of the dark after that and felt as though a great burden had lifted from me. I believe I had the experience because I was so frightened of the dark.'

As I've said before even if it were all in the mind such experiences are enriching. But occasionally a child's guardian helper can be seen or heard by an adult. I assume that fifteen-month-old Carl was too young to know he had a guardian - but maybe he did. His mum Sue had an old labrador called Kim that had died just before Carl was born. Kim had loved children. Sue thought she'd sensed the dog around the baby and had once seen a black shadow lying at the bottom of the cot but dismissed it as imagination.

'One day Sue heard urgent barking outside the window while she was busy in the kitchen and was convinced it was Kim who used to bark exactly like that when something was wrong. But she could see nothing. The urgent barking continued and now seemed to be coming from round the corner of the house. Afraid a stray dog might have got in as she'd left Carl in his play-pen by the open lounge window Sue rushed towards the front garden just in time to see baby Carl about to toddle through the gate which someone had unlocked. Carl had dragged a coffee table to the outside of the playpen, hauled himself up and made a bid for freedom. The barking stopped and Sue never heard it again. Coincidence, maternal instinct or a loved family pet keeping an eye on the baby? Carl never talked about an invisible dog when he grew older though a picture of the dog became one of his treasures.

It is important that the psychic world is discussed like any other subject and children are allowed to ask any questions without fear of ridicule. We tend to be more unwilling to bring the psychic into the open than to talk about sex with our youngsters. Yet many an adolescent ignorant of the psychological and psychic impact of dabbling has 'scared herself almost to death' and felt unable to confide in adults.

Pam had tried to talk to her mum about ghosts because she was fascinated by the subject but her mother told her the psychic was rubbish. When Pam was 14 she started to use the ouija board at school with her friends. Pam was specially singled out for nice messages to her friends' annoyance and they accused her of cheating. The spirit told her she'd meet a new boyfriend called John (not unlikely since she was probably giving out friendly vibes to every John within a hundred miles).

The spirit also promised she'd do well in her end of term exams. Pam had worked hard all year but was convinced that her success was due to the board.

Then Pam was told by the glass she had a great psychic gift so she started to play with lexicon letters at home alone. But things turned nasty. The spirit said her best friend Jan was jealous and saying nasty things behind her back. Pam caught Jan whispering to another girl in the cloakroom and after a terrible row they stopped speaking. Then the glass warned her that if she went dancing there would be a fire at the disco that would disfigure her face.

The spirit refused to say when this would happen so she gave up going to discos even at school. The next week the spirit told her the school bus would crash but again gave no time limit. Pam was terrified and refused to go to school.

Her mum, seeing Pam behaving strangely, finally confronted her and asked if she had been taking drugs. Pam confessed what she'd been doing and her mother called in the local priest. They destroyed the cards and blessed her bedroom. Pam's mother felt very guilty that she'd not allowed her daughter to talk about the psychic when she was first interested and that she'd found it easier to suspect her of taking drugs rather than dabbling in the occult. Teenage experiments are very common and it's only by bringing the psychic out into the open that its darker aspects can lose any mystique and glamour.

Of course it's far easier to acknowledge the psychic world if you're rich and powerful. For generations Joan Penelope Cope's family had lived in Bramshill House in Berkshire (now a high-powered college for police officers on the fast track for promotion). She claimed to have seen dozens of ghosts. Her memoirs from the age of 12 in 1938 which she had published privately are full of accounts of the ghosts she and her younger brother and mother saw.

Even in her pram, she writes, she would talk about 'green man', a creature reputed to appear in the shrubbery. Her childhood was filled with ghosts as she played in the old rooms and the extensive grounds. When she was seven a ghost came to her room one night. 'I found myself gazing at a youngish woman who must have once been quite good-looking—even a beauty, but death had deprived her of her charms ——her eyes were black with a kind of dead light in them.' Her brother saw the ghost too in his room.

She wrote: ' "Oh Joan," he said. "I saw the lady." And all the thousand questions I pounded on him he simply and quietly answered "just the same."

'Fairies were part of one's daily life. I never remember having the slightest doubt as to their reality and I'm not at all sure I was not right.'

The children according to Joan's account of her childhood were brought up with Mummer plays at Christmas, dressing up in Georgian costumes and listening to legends of heroic deeds at night round log fires beneath portraits of esteemed ancestors who smiled down on them.

Then Joan's beloved nanny was sent away when Joan was nine and the children made a moping corner 'with a photo and altar to pray for her'. But it was a battle for the children to hold on to their magical world. Joan reported that the new governess 'strove to do away with our fairy kingdom - But though we gradually silenced out, I kept up my imagination firmly to myself'.

The family ghosts became friends of the children though as he grew older Anthony was less enthusiastic. 'Oh Joan you know I can't see this kind of thing like you do.'

But Joan continued to rub shoulders with the unseen past till the house was sold. When visitors came she would try to alert them to the ghosts that were mingling with the invited guests. 'Look, there's Sir John Cope, the fifth baronet but he's not alone. There are hundreds and hundreds of them and the air's stifling just like in a crowd.'

Of course ghosts may find it easier to appear where they are accepted as part of the furnishings and hence Joan really did see crowds of them. Also there is a limit to the number of phantoms you can cram in to the average semi.

But it's not easy if you are poor and depend on welfare benefits. Children's psychic experiences can set off unwarranted alarm bells. Tina phoned me because her young daughter Julie had mentioned to her teacher that she was seeing people in her bedroom at their council flat at night, talking and selling things. Tina was a single parent living on social security and alarm bells rang. In fact Tina knew no one and spent all her time either at home with her daughter or at work while Julie was at school.

A social worker had come round for a chat but didn't stay long after Julie started describing the old-fashioned people pushing barrows, since the flat was on the sixth floor. It was suggested that Julie might benefit from seeing a child psychologist. Julie's stories were put down as compensatory fantasies because she lacked a father figure and before long she stopped talking about the people. But for a long time Tina had more than her share of professional visits.

So why did Tina phone me? Because like many people she wanted reassurance that her daughter wasn't odd or psychologically disturbed. When Tina mentioned the name of the street she lived in was Market Street, though the flats were built in the nineteen sixties I suggested she asked at the local library about the history of the area.

Next day she rang back to tell me that until the last war when most of the buildings were flattened there had been a street market in the area. Did I suggest she contacted social services to explain the mystery? As I said it's easier to have your word accepted if you live in a big house like Bramshill.

The ghosts, the family secret, as Janet Boucher, the child psychiatrist, calls it, that mother and children share a psychic world was in a big powerful household no real problem, though the governess was not too happy. It would seem that to be rich or powerful does make it more possible to acknowledge ghosts without being called cranky. In more ordinary families, mum and the children often keep their psychic experiences secret from the outside world and sometimes from dad, which can have all sorts of implications for the family chemistry. Those who do see ghosts, quickly come to learn that it is not acceptable to admit this generally, so they have to hide what is a valid part of their lives or risk being labelled as odd.

Some psychologists say mum feeds into the child's already receptive mind the message: 'It's OK to be psychic.' This is seen to be acceptable if a child's fantasy world is left behind as a normal developmental stage. It can seen by psychologists as a power ploy by mum or the child to exclude dad, especially if mum is lonely and wants to hang on to the child. At school, where the majority of children are non-psychic, the world either fades or goes underground.

There would seem to be a gender issues as well. Do boys grow out of this stage or at least keep it under wraps even from the family, whereas the girl can think 'Mum's psychic so its OK for me to be psychic when I'm grown up' and so it carries on from generation to generation almost ritualistically.

251

The Cope's rituals ended with the sale of their grand house and today it belongs to the Home Office. Despite the blocks of flats which have been built in the wooded grounds and Whitehall's 'improvements' to the property it still retains the magic which influenced the young Miss Cope so deeply.

I toured it one evening with my husband as the guest of a friend from the police and we were regaled with stories of various ghosts said to stalk the stately home with no respect for the forces of law and order now settled there. As we stood on the grand terrace staring out across the fields in the twilight I was shaken to see white forms approaching us, gliding over the ground. Ghosts! I thought immediately.

The figures were not ghosts but a herd of rare white deer, kept in the house grounds. It was a vivid example of how the power of suggestion can work.

We do not know how many children see — for want of better words — ghosts, angels or goblins or what proportion of these are fantasy or psychic phenomena.

Neither can we be sure if, the child has seen something from another world, if he or she is describing it correctly or in terms which come closest to his or her limited experience.

As I have related, Jack once told me that he had seen an 'enormous panda bear' in the New Forest which turned out to be a large black and white cow.

A child who does see some sort of shining messenger from heaven may well translate this in terms of the tinsel-winged angels he or she has been taught to expect.

We do know that may small children can read their

parents minds and that at birth, as junior is pushing his way into this world, poor old mum can be whisked off to some pretty strange places after which she may never be quite the same again.

But what we don't know (though I would love to find out) is how many perfectly ordinary families do have a ghost or childhood psychic event in family folklore that is brought out only on family occasions, but not shared with the outside world.

Though some psychologists and psychiatrists are very nervous about it, the psychic world of the normal child has much to teach them about family stress and the child's way of coping with it.

Parents also need to learn to cope with a child's contact with the paranormal. Children can be damaged if their experiences are ridiculed or dismissed. Every experience and fear has to be discussed in a caring and open-minded way. Even if the experience is patently not paranormal, it is real to the child and could be affecting his or her sense of well-being.

If it is psychic, then it casts a new insight on to our mundane world. Should psychic powers be encouraged? A tricky question when it is difficult enough to cultivate the normal abilities a child possesses.

We do not know the extent of the psychic world and in attempting to do more than appreciate those rare glimpses we get could distort it, or give it a place in children's lives where they feel either obliged to perform, or afraid of what would seem to be a natural ability that sometimes fades or lies dormant, perhaps until the child's own infant reopens the door.

Perhaps all we can do is give the child time and space and a caring and supportive environment.

Today there are many commercial pressures which bear down on the spiritual lives of our children (in the fullest sense of spiritual which embraces more than the psychic world or church-going). Proper values often take second place to a shiny new bike and the latest video games. Perhaps we should deal with this before trying to tackle new frontiers.

But all too soon the magic years are gone. We have stuffed their heads with potted fantasy that I fear will be cold comfort as age takes us all back to the place from which we all began.

Children's psychic experiences can give us an insight into a world we have forgotten. We do not know where fantasy ends and the psychic begins or if indeed there is such a boundary. Maybe angels really do have golden wings and dead grannies can come back to keep an eye on a sick or sad grandchild.

It may be that our perceptions of reality are dulled by the material world and the thousand and one worries that narrow our horizons. Yet if we stop and share the magical world of our children we may for a moment see fairies again and know as we once did that the universe will end with a hug and a happy ever after and not a big bang.

Finally, do you want your child to be able to monitor your every thought? Or, worse still, as telepathy is a two-way process to have their incessant chatter running through your mind without respite?

Or supposing you had a premonition every time your child was going to fall over in the playground or get bopped by one of his friends? What do you do? Write a note to school saying: 'Please excuse my child from play this week as he might fall off the climbing frame at a quarter to one next Thursday?'

Worst of all, supposing they could take off in their astral bodies? It's hard enough getting the real body to bed without having an astral form popping down to watch the late night film with you.

It would play havoc with discipline: 'Jack, will you get back in your body at once!'

And that last resort, 'Get to your room and stay there', would be meaningless. The physical body might obey but five minutes later the astral form would be whizzing round at the playground in the local park.

Cassandra Eason is always pleased to hear from readers about their experiences and tries to reply to all letters. She can be contacted through her publishers